R. Lemming

The

MAINSPRING

of Human Progress

BY

HENRY GRADY WEAVER

THE FOUNDATION FOR
ECONOMIC EDUCATION, INC.
IRVINGTON-ON-HUDSON, NEW YORK

1953

TABLE OF CONTENTS

PART FOUR—FRUITS OF FREEDOM

APPENDIX

THE AUTHOR AND THE BOOK

Henry Grady Weaver was born at Eatonton, Georgia, December 24, 1889. He received his B.S. from Georgia Tech in 1911, and held a series of jobs in various phases of the automobile industry until 1921. That was the year he went with General Motors. He soon became head of its Customer Research Staff and was judged of sufficient importance in his field to be the Time *magazine "cover man" for its issue of November 14, 1938.*

Time said of "Buck" Weaver: "He dresses with studied informality—slouch hat, tweedy, sloppy suit. He is short, bow-legged, has Clark Gable ears and hair cropped short. . . .

"Jittery as a terrier, he cannot sit still, swivels between two desks, hops up to flip some papers, peers through a cloud of smoke with his one good eye (he has been blind in his right eye since birth). Likable and expansive, he talks incessantly, wrinkles his nose when amused, which is often."

Mr. Weaver, a Baptist, was married in 1923 (two children). He is the author of many articles on psychological research. Convinced that human liberty is the mainspring of progress— and that government tends always to tyranny—he decided to popularize these themes for the American people. His first major effort was this book, Mainspring. *In it he said: "If the book meets with a reasonable reception, I plan to do the same sort of thing with other books. For example, I'd like to reinterpret the writings of Frederic Bastiat in the language of today and from the American viewpoint. I'd like to develop a dramatization of the all-but-forgotten* Federalist Papers.*"*

His Mainspring *proved a tremendous success, but Henry Grady Weaver died on January 3, 1949.*

In addition to keeping his book in print, the Foundation for Economic Education hopes to accomplish some of the other vitally-needed jobs that Mr. Weaver had mapped out for himself.

First published in 1947 by Talbot Books, some 220,000 copies of Mainspring *have been printed.*

In an "author's notation" in the first printing of the book, Mr. Weaver states: "In some respects, Mainspring *is a condensation of Rose Wilder Lane's book,* The Discovery of Freedom. *In other respects, it is an amplification. Inspired by her thesis and with her gracious consent, I've tried to retell her story in my own way, making liberal use of her material —plus ideas growing out of personal experiences and gathered from various sources. Mrs. Lane should not be blamed for any omissions, deviations, and additions. (She does not always agree with me—and vice versa!)"*

During one of his visits with us here at the Foundation, Mr. Weaver mentioned the fact that some of his statements had been challenged by readers of his book, and that he intended to make a few minor revisions in the third printing of it. We ourselves offered criticisms and suggestions to Mr. Weaver on a few of these disputed points. He agreed in some instances and noted them for change. Unfortunately, his untimely death occurred before another printing. In the few instances where we recall his agreement, we have taken the liberty of making the changes as discussed with him.

An index has been added to this edition. A new format and type-face have been selected, and the book has been edited in conformity with our own house style — The University of Chicago Press Manual of Style.

> *Leonard E. Read*
> *of the Foundation Staff*

Part I

COMPARISONS AND CONTRASTS

Chapter 1

PUZZLING QUESTIONS
OF VITAL CONCERN TO
2,155,000,000 INDIVIDUALS

FOR 60 known centuries, this planet that we call Earth has been inhabited by human beings not much different from ourselves. Their desire to live has been just as strong as ours. They have had at least as much physical strength as the average person of today, and among them have been men and women of great intelligence. But down through the ages, most human beings have gone hungry, and many have always starved.

The ancient Assyrians, Persians, Egyptians, and Greeks were intelligent people; but in spite of their intelligence and their fertile lands, they were never able to get enough to eat. They often killed their babies because they couldn't feed them.

The Roman Empire collapsed in famine. The French were dying of hunger when Thomas Jefferson was President of the United States. As late as 1846, the Irish were starving to death; and no one was particularly surprised because famines in the Old World were the rule rather than the exception. It is only within the last century that western Europeans have had enough food to keep them alive — soup and bread in France, fish in Scandinavia, beef in England.

Hunger has always been normal. Even to this day,

famines kill multitudes in China, India, Africa; and in the 1930's, thousands upon thousands starved to death on the richest farmlands of the Soviet Union.

Down through the ages, countless millions, struggling unsuccessfully to keep bare life in wretched bodies, have died young in misery and squalor. Then suddenly, in one spot on this planet, people eat so abundantly that the pangs of hunger are forgotten.

The Questions

Why did men die of starvation for 6,000 years? Why is it that we in America have never had a famine?

Why did men walk and carry goods (and other men) on their straining backs for 6,000 years — then suddenly, on only a small part of the earth's surface, the forces of nature are harnessed to do the bidding of the humblest citizen?

Why did families live for 6,000 years in caves and floorless hovels, without windows or chimneys — then within a few generations, we in America take floors, rugs, chairs, tables, windows, and chimneys for granted and regard electric lights, refrigerators, running water, porcelain baths, and toilets as common necessities?

Why did men, women, and children eke out their meager existence for 6,000 years, toiling desperately from dawn to dark — barefoot, half-naked, unwashed, unshaved, uncombed, with lousy hair, mangy skins, and rotting teeth — then suddenly, in one place on earth there is an abundance of such things as rayon underwear, nylon hose, shower baths, safety razors, ice cream sodas, lipsticks, and permanent waves?

[12]

What Are the Answers?

It's incredible, if we would but pause to reflect! Swiftly, in less than a hundred years, Americans have conquered the darkness of night — from pine knots and candles to kerosene lamps, to gas jets; then to electric bulbs, neon lights, fluorescent tubes.

We have created wholly new and astounding defenses against weather — from fireplaces to stoves, furnaces, automatic burners, insulation, air conditioning.

We are conquering pain and disease, prolonging life, and resisting death itself — with anesthetics, surgery, sanitation, hygiene, dietetics.

We have made stupendous attacks on space — from ox-carts, rafts, and canoes to railroads, steamboats, streetcars, subways, automobiles, trucks, busses, airplanes — and attacks on time through telegraph, telephone, and radio.

We have moved from backbreaking drudgery into the modern age of power, substituting steam, electricity, and gasoline for the brawn of man; and today the nuclear physicist is taking over and finding ways for subduing to human uses the infiinitesimally tiny atom — tapping a new source of power so vast that it bids fair to dwarf anything that has gone before.

It is true that many of these developments originated in other countries. But new ideas are of little value in raising standards of living unless and until something is done about them. The plain fact is that we in America have outdistanced the world in extending the benefits of inventions and discoveries to the vast majority of people in all walks of life.

How Did It Happen?

Three generations — grandfather to grandson — have created these wonders which surpass the utmost imaginings of all previous time. How did it come about? How can it be explained? Just what has been responsible for this unprecedented burst of progress, which has so quickly transformed a hostile wilderness into the most prosperous and advanced country that the world has ever known?

Perhaps the best way to find the answer is first to rule out some of the factors that were *not* responsible.

To say that it is because of our natural resources is hardly enough. The same rich resources were here when the mound builders held forth. Americans have had no monopoly on iron, coal, copper, aluminum, zinc, lead, or other materials. Such things have always been available to human beings. China, India, Russia, Africa — all have great natural resources. Crude oil oozed from the earth in Baku 4,000 years ago; and when Julius Caesar marched west into Gaul, Europe was a rich and virgin wilderness inhabited by a few roving savages, much as America was when the Pilgrim Fathers landed at Plymouth.*

Is it because we work harder? Again the answer is "No" because in most countries the people work much harder, on the average, than we do.

*Really, when you come right down to it, nothing is a "natural resource" until after men have made it useful to human beings. Coal was not a natural resource to Julius Caesar, nor crude oil to Alexander the Great, nor aluminum to Ben Franklin, nor the atom to anyone until 1945. Men may discover uses for any substance. Nobody can know today what may be a natural resource tomorrow. It is not natural resources, but the uses men make of them that really count.

[14]

Can it be that we are a people of inherent superiority? That sounds fine in after-dinner oratory and goes over big at election time, but the argument is difficult to support. Our own ancestors, including the Anglo-Saxons, have starved right along with everyone else.

Can it be that we have more energy than other peoples of the world? That's not the answer either, but it's getting pretty close. We are not endowed with any superior energy — mental or physical — but it is a fact that we, in the United States of America, have made more effective use of our human energies than have any other people on the face of the globe — anywhere or at any time.

The Real Answer

That's the answer — the real answer — the only answer. It's a very simple answer, perhaps too simple to be readily accepted. So it is the purpose of this book to dig beneath the surface and to seek the reasons underlying the reason.

In other words, just why does human energy work better here than anywhere else? And answering that question leads us into a whole string of questions, such as:

1. What is the nature of human energy?
2. How does it differ from other forms of energy?
3. What makes it work?
4. What are the things that keep it from working?
5. How can it be made to work better? more efficiently? more effectively?

The answers, even the partial answers, to these questions

[15]

should be extremely helpful in contributing to future progress.

In the last analysis, poverty, famine, and the devastations of war are all traceable to a lack of understanding of human energy and to a failure to use it to the best advantage.

History affords abundant evidence in support of that statement; but the evidence is somewhat obscured because most of the textbooks stress war and conflict, rather than the causes of war and what might be done to prevent war.*

In later chapters, we'll attempt to reverse the usual procedure. In other words, we'll try to see what can be learned from history as bearing upon the effective use of human energy, which advances progress — as against the misuse of human energy, which retards progress and leads to the destruction of life as well as wealth. But as a background for the main text of this book, it seems necessary, first of all, to review a few elementary facts — including a lot of things which we already know but which we are inclined to overlook.

Energy

First, let's consider the general subject of energy — human versus nonhuman. This entire planet is made up of energy. The atoms of air surrounding it are energy. The sun pours energy upon this air and upon this earth. Life depends on energy; in fact, life *is* energy.

*From a standpoint of military history, I suppose it's important to know that the Battle of Bull Run came ahead of Vicksburg, but Margaret Mitchell's *Gone With the Wind* is far more revealing as bearing upon the causes and effects of the War Between the States.

Every living thing must struggle for its existence, and human beings are no exception. The thin defenses of civilization tend to obscure the stark realities; but men and women survive on this earth only because their energies constantly convert other forms of energy to satisfy human needs, and constantly attack the nonhuman energies that are dangerous to human existence.

Some people are keenly aware of this: doctors and nurses, farmers, sailors, construction engineers, weather forecasters, telephone linemen, airplane pilots, railroad men, "sand hogs," miners — all the fighters who protect human life and keep the modern world existing. Such people stand the brunt of the struggle and enable the rest of us to forget.

But it is important that we do not forget. When we do forget, there is the temptation to indulge in wishful thinking — to build imaginative Utopias on the basis of things as we might like them to be, instead of facing the real human situation and reckoning with things as they are. In the last analysis, there can be no progress except through the more effective use of our individual energies, personal initiatives, and imaginative abilities — applied to the things and forces of nature.

Energy at Work

But let's get away from broad generalities for a moment and take a closer look at human energy at work.

Right now you are reading this book. Let's say you want to turn a page. You are the dynamo that generates the energy to turn the page. Your brain-energy makes the decision and controls the movement of the muscle-pulleys and bone-levers of your arm, your hand, and your fingers; and you turn the page.

The energy that you used to turn the page is the same kind of energy that created this book. Down through centuries of time and across space, from the first maker of paper, of ink, of type, every act of the innumerable minds and hands that created this book and delivered it to you — miners digging coal and iron in Pennsylvania, woodsmen sinking their axes into spruce in Norway and Oregon, chemists in laboratories, workers in factories and foundries, mechanics, printers, binders — was an operation of human energy generated and controlled by the person who performed the act.

And that's really shortchanging the story. To make it complete, we would have to go back to the thousands of people who invented the tools — not just the paper-making machinery and the printing presses and binding equipment, but the tools that were used to make all these things, plus the tools that were used to make the tools.

As a result of modern equipment and facilities, this copy of this book was produced and delivered to you at a cost of less than an hour of human time, whereas a few hundred years ago it would have taken months.

It all comes back to the effective use of human energy; and human energy, like any other energy, operates according to certain natural laws. For one thing, it works only under its own natural control. Your decision to turn the page released the energy to turn it. It was your will which controlled the use of that energy. Nothing else *can* control it.

It is true, of course, that many of your actions are prompted by suggestions and requests or orders and commands from others; but that doesn't change the fact that the decision to act and the action itself are always under your own control.

Freedom and Responsibility

Let's take an extreme case. A robber breaks into your house and threatens you at the point of a gun. Discretion being the better part of valor, you give in and tell him where your valuables are hidden. But *you* make the decision, and *you* do the telling.

If, instead of a robber, it were a kidnaper after your child, it would be a different story. But in either case, your thoughts and acts are under your own control. Thousands of men and women have suffered torture and even death without speaking a word that their persecutors tried to make them speak.

Your freedom of action may be forbidden, restricted, or prevented by force. The robber, kidnaper, or jailer may bind your hands and feet and put a gag in your mouth. But the fact remains that no amount of force can *make* you act unless you agree — perhaps with hesitation and regret — to do so.

I know this all sounds hairsplitting and academic, but it leads to a very important point — in fact, to two important points:

1. Individual freedom is the natural heritage of each living person.
2. Freedom cannot be separated from responsibility.

Your natural freedom — your control over your own life-energy — was born in you along with life itself. It is a part of life itself. No one can give it to you, nor can you give it to someone else. Nor can you hold any other person responsible for your acts. Control simply can't be separated from responsibility; control *is* responsibility.

Results versus Desires

A steam engine will not run on gasoline, nor will a gasoline engine run on steam.

To use any kind of energy effectively, it is first necessary to understand the nature of the energy and then to set up conditions that will permit it to work to the best advantage.

To make the most effective use of steam energy, it is necessary to reckon with the nature of steam. To make the most effective use of human energy, it is necessary to reckon with the nature of man. And there's no escaping the fact that human energy operates very differently from any other energy.

Steam energy always acts in exactly the same way, so long as the conditions are the same — ditto gasoline energy and electrical energy.

Insects and animals follow certain patterns of action. Honeybees, for example, all make the same hexagonal cells of wax. Beavers all build the same form of dam, and the same kinds of birds make the same kinds of nests. Generation after generation, they continue to follow their changeless routines — always doing the same things in the same ways.

But a man is different because he is a human being; and as a human being, he has the power of reason, the power of imagination, the ability to capitalize on the experiences of the past and the present as bearing on the problems of the future. He has the ability to change *himself* as well as his environment. He has the ability to progress and to keep on progressing.

Plants occupy space and contend with each other for it. Animals defend their possession of places and things. But man has enormous powers, of unknown extent, to make new things and to change old things into new forms. He not only owns property, but he also actually creates property.

In the last analysis, a thing is not property unless it is owned; and without ownership, there is little incentive to improve it.

Chapter 2

THE GREAT MULTIPLIER

THROUGH foresight, imagination, and individual initiative, man develops tools and facilities which expand his efforts and enable him to produce things which would not otherwise be possible. This is an outstanding difference between man and animal, just as it is an outstanding difference between civilization and barbarism.

Progress toward better living would never have been possible, except through the development of tools to extend the uses of human energy — tools that harness the forces of nature as a substitute for muscular effort.

The American Economic Foundation puts it in terms of the mathematical equation $MMP = NR + HE \times T$, which is just a shorthand way of saying that "man's material progress *depends on* natural resources *plus* human energy *multiplied by* tools." That's a neat way to express it, and the formula is worth remembering. But no amount of mathematics can ever tell the real story.

Let's go back about 500,000 years and look in on one of our Stone Age ancestors. Here, squatting in front of his cave, is a man with a new idea. He's one of the real pioneer inventors. He's on the verge of inventing the first tool — or *almost* the first tool. Clubs have long been used for fighting, and sharp, jagged stones have probably been used for cutting and hacking. But our neolithic genius is going to combine the two ideas by fastening a sharp stone onto the end of a club or a handle, thus increasing the momentum and the force of impact. He's going to create a new tool — a crude sort of ax.

Without Tools

All he has to work with are the general idea and the raw materials — plus the energy and the will power to do a job. Without any tools, it's going to take about a week of steady work — except that he won't be able to work on it steadily. He'll have to take time out to hunt for his food.

Perhaps he could have persuaded someone else to do that for him, but it's rather doubtful because, mind you, this was back in the early Stone Age; and it seems reasonable to assume that the general practice of exchanging goods and services came *after* the invention of tools.

Of course, if he'd been sick and unable to forage for his own food, the others might have understood and helped him; but for a strong, healthy man to waste his time fooling around with sticks and stones was downright lunacy. He should have been out hunting birds' eggs, or catching luscious grasshoppers, or indulging in a spree down near the river bank where the ground was covered with slightly fermented mulberries.

So, instead of anyone's bringing him food, it's more likely that his family and friends just laughed at him. Aided and abetted by the witch doctors, they may have gone so far as to sabotage his early efforts.

The same sort of thing had probably happened to his forerunners. Maybe that's why the making of an ax had been so long delayed. Surely, the same idea must have occurred to many others before him.

[23]

But right now, we are talking about the fellow who has the tenacity to buck the tide of public opinion and get the job done. Of course, after the ax is finished, things will take a different turn. He'll be able to demonstrate its advantages; and from then on, he can swap the loan of his ax for food, furs, and feathers. Maybe he'll be able to put in his whole time making more and better axes — and there's lots of room for improvement.

The first crude ax was nothing to brag about; but it was an important forward-looking step, and it typifies the kind of thinking that sets man completely apart from the animals, the birds, and the bees.

Triple Effect

It takes very little imagination to see how the invention of this crude hand tool led to the development of other tools and to the creation of various other things — rafts, houses, wheels, etc. But the main point is that the introduction of tools marked the beginning of man's progress in three important directions:

1. More effective use of energy.

2. Specialization of effort.

3. Advances in human co-operation and improvements in living conditions, through the peaceful exchange of goods and services.

Also, the introduction of tools brought into sharper focus the importance of individual property rights. Unless a person has a chance of gaining some direct benefit from his extra efforts, there is not much inducement for him to think ahead and to make the sacrifices necessary to provide the tools of production. And without the tools of production, human beings would sink back into a state of barbarism.

We have moved a long way from the Stone Age, and today almost everyone depends for his welfare — for his very life — upon exchanges of ownership.

Chapter 3

NETWORKS AND PITFALLS

THE modern world is an intricate network of living human energies linking all persons in co-operative effort and in one common fate. The Turks have bread because the Americans smoke cigarettes. New Yorkers eat pineapple ripened in Hawaii because the Burmese mine tin. We drink coffee at breakfast because Brazilians need our iron, machinery, and wheat. And Japanese babies grow strong and healthy when American women buy silk lingerie.

This is the kind of world in which men and women naturally want to live. And it is the kind of world they begin to create when they are free to use their individual energies and are free to co-operate among themselves — voluntarily.

Thus the brotherhood of man is not an ideal of selflessness which human beings are too sinful to achieve. It is stern reality. All persons are bound together in the one imperative desire to survive. *Do unto others as you would have them do unto you* is not only a sound moral precept, it is also the hardheaded advice of practical self-interest. Whoever injures another injures himself because he decreases the opportunities for gain that come through co-operation and exchange.

But how can we reconcile the principle of co-operation with the conflicts of competition? The answer is that there is nothing inconsistent between the two. Competition is the practical manifestation of human beings in free control of their individual affairs arriving at a balance in their relationships with one another. Free competition is, within itself, a co-operative process.

Competitive bargaining, for example, is essential to equitable transactions. The buyer wants a lower price; the seller wants a higher price. This may give rise to conflict and argument. But the temporary period of debate that may precede the exchange of goods and services is in no sense contradictory to the co-operative relationships underlying the whole idea of exchange. Nor are the conflicts and rivalries of opposing viewpoints confined to the market place. They are found in the home, the church, the club, the schoolroom, the playground — everywhere.

Eternal Dilemma

Since the uses of human energy are innumerable — and since there is wide variation in tastes and desires — individual persons, left to their own volition, rarely choose to do the same things in the same way at the same time. All friends, lovers, playmates, family groups, business associates have experienced the dilemma in varying degrees: Shall we stay at home or go to the movies? Shall we listen to the symphony or to the soap opera? Shall we plant alfalfa or peanuts? Shall we buy or build this or that?

Life is a continuous series of conflicts and compromises; and, generally speaking, the co-operative actions growing out of such conflicts and compromises are sounder than if each one of us were able to carry out his own ideas, in his own way and without regard for anyone else.

[27]

But from the viewpoint of the individual, it sometimes appears that the efforts of others are unnecessary obstacles to his own direct action in achieving his own personal desires. Thus, it occurs to him that maybe there should be some centralized control or overriding authority to govern all human energies as a unit. This concept has a strong appeal because lurking beneath it is the alluring assumption that the *right* kind of authority would direct the affairs of all mankind in harmony with the individual's own personal views — thus relieving him of the trouble and responsibility of making his own ideas work.

Just by way of illustration, let's suppose I have an idea; and while we're at it, let's make it something really big.

Let's assume that I have a plan or a program which would, in my opinion, improve the lot of all mankind — especially that portion of mankind that's in the same position as I. I'm completely sold on the virtues of my idea. But there are those who disagree. I get tired of trying to persuade them. There ought to be an easier and a quicker way. I'm feeling a bit frustrated; and in bolstering my ego, I forget that others are entitled to have different views. I conclude that coercion is the only way, and I find comfort in the reassuring alibi, *the end justifies the means.*

Rationalization

But so much for the background. Now let's eavesdrop while I lull my conscience and build up my own case in my own mind, to wit:

No one can doubt my sincerity, and I'm wholly unselfish in my motives — or at least *almost* wholly unselfish. I don't stand to make any money out of it — at least not much — and anyway, the total benefits to others will far outweigh the benefits to me. Naturally, I'll get some honor and glory; but after all, it *is* my idea. . . .

Those of my friends who are in the same position as I am understand all this, and they agree with me — or at least *most* of them do. But what about these others — the ones who seem determined to block my efforts? It's true that my program would cost them a little money at the start; but in the long run, everybody would be better off, including them. . . .

The trouble is that they are nonprogressive and downright selfish; but they aren't honest enough to come out and admit it. They contend that my plan has certain shortcomings. Well, what of it? Sure, there may be a few things that need to be ironed out, but why not get started and worry about the details later on? The advantages would more than offset any minor defects, and there's been too much delay already. . . .

This is the Atomic Age, and the human race must no longer be deprived of the benefits that I am ready to bring it. Those who don't see the light must be *made* to see the light. I'm not going to compromise my principles by giving in to a bunch of self-seeking reactionaries. They've got to be forced into line, and that calls for government assistance. (There ought to be a law!) If we had the *right kind of people* in government, they'd have stepped in and supported my cause long ago. That's what governments are for. . . .

What we need is a stronger government, run by men who would turn a deaf ear to the kind of folks who are blocking my program. There's been too much compromising, too much dillydallying. It's about time we had a new form of government — a more progressive government, run on truly democratic principles but with enough power to get things under control and really do a job. Maybe we ought to have a "strong man at the helm" — not a despot, mind you, but a truly beneficent dictator — one who would have the real interests of the real people at heart; one smart enough to run things the way I know they ought to be run. . . .

And maybe, just to be on the safe side, it ought to be *me!*

That concludes the example. I agree that it is a bit extreme — or, to say the least, it is rather bluntly presented. Few people would consciously try to force the entire world into line with their own pet ideas. But almost every individual, at one time or another, gets the feeling that there should be some kind of centralized authority which would control human energies as a unit and "run things the way they ought to be run."

There's nothing new in the idea. Since the beginning of recorded history on down through the present time, it has captured the imaginations of people everywhere, in all walks of life. Of course, different individuals have different views as to just how things ought to be run, but the idea persists that there should be a unified control; and each proponent, in his own imagination and with the best of intentions, fondly visualizes the kind of control that would favor his own personal ideas.

Among the learned philosophers, the age-old problem has been to determine just who or what is in control, or should be in control, of living persons. From Plato to Spengler, the problem has been to identify the authority

— and then to turn over to it all the troubles of the human race.

At one time or another, every conceivable form of authority has been tried, but each has failed for the simple reasons that:

1. Only an individual human being can generate human energy.
2. Only an individual human being can control the energy he generates.

The lack of understanding of these simple, basic truths has, for over 6,000 years, stagnated human progress and kept the vast majority of people underfed, poorly clothed, embroiled in wars, and dying from famine and pestilence.

Foundation of Faith

In the following chapters, we shall briefly review the various types of authority and try to appraise their results in terms of human good. The best way to go at it is first to consider the religious beliefs which underlie the different kinds of authority, political structure, or what is generally called government.

I am using the word *religious* in its broad sense, but I think it can be shown that any form of human organization, whether it be political, commercial, or social, reflects the deep-seated faith of the people who organize it and keep it going. Individuals direct their energies and build their organizations according to their views of reality — what they conceive to be desirable and good.

Every human act is preceded by a decision to act, and that decision is based on faith. One cannot even think without a deep-seated faith that he exists and that there is a supreme standard of good in the universe. This is true of every living person — whether his god is the God of Abraham and Christ, Zeus or Isis, reason or fate, history or astrology, or any other god, whether it be true or false.

When the belief is false, the result will be different from what was expected. But the fact remains that every action of every human being springs from the desire to attain something which he considers to be good — or from the desire to avoid something which he thinks is evil or undesirable.

Since the actions of any individual are determined by his beliefs, it follows that the underlying control of the energies of any group of persons is the religious faith prevailing among them.

There are hundreds, if not thousands, of variations in religious faith; but for purposes of this discussion, they all may be grouped under three general headings:

1. The pagan view, a fatalistic belief in the mythical gods — the will-of-the-mass, the all-powerful earthly ruler or living authority.

2. The nonpagan view, as reflected in the Hebrew, the Christian, and the Moslem faiths.

3. Compromises between the two, as typified by the feudal system.

Just what are the basic differences in these views? How do they affect the uses of human energy? What are the results in terms of progress — spiritual as well as material? What do these three religious views mean to you and to me as bearing on the present and the future?

PART II

THE OLD WORLD VIEWS

Chapter 4

THE PAGAN VIEW

THE pagan has a fatalistic outlook on life. He believes that the individual is helpless; that he is wholly at the mercy of relentless forces outside of himself; that there's nothing he can do to improve his lot.

The vast majority of people have always been pagans. Most of them are still pagans. The superstition is deep-seated. It had its beginning back in prehistoric times.

Mythology tells how special gods were in charge of everything affecting human life. Some gods controlled thunder; some controlled lightning; some controlled rain. Others controlled the seasons, the bounty of the harvest, the multiplication of the flocks, and the birth of children.

There were sun-gods, love-gods, gods of jealousy, gods of hatred, and gods of war. Whimsical and prankish gods looked after everything. All that man could do was to keep peace with them by making such sacrifices, human and otherwise, as were dictated by tribal custom.

In ancient times, the pagan gods and goddesses were known by various names — Zeus, Isis, Osiris, Eros, Jupiter, Juno, Apollo, Venus, Mercury, Diana, Neptune, Pluto, Mars. In modern times, they are given more modern names, but the underlying idea is the same.

From the pagan viewpoint, man is not self-controlling, not responsible for his own acts. The pagan universe is timeless, changeless, static. There is no such thing as progress. Any apparent change is merely a human illusion. Man is passive. His place is fixed. He has no freedom of will. His fate is decreed. If he tries to resist, his efforts will be futile.

The pagan belief is similar to that of a very young child. The newborn babe has not yet learned how to control himself. He must be spanked before he can even breathe, and for a long time he will kick himself in the eye when he tries to taste his toes. He cannot get food; he is fed. He is uncomfortable, and he is turned over. Warmth, comfort, cleanliness — all are given to him by some power outside himself, enormously stronger than he. This power controls the *conditions* of his life, but it does not control *him*. Did you ever try to stop a baby's squalling when he merely wanted to squall?

If babies were able to think and speak, no doubt any baby — all babies — would contend that some great power controls the lives of babies. But babies grow up, and in time the normal baby becomes a self-controlling human being. Yet, throughout all history, down to and including modern times, few adult persons have ever discovered that they are really free.

An Ancient Superstition

Most human beings cling to the ancient superstition that they are not self-controlling and not responsible for their own acts. For thousands of years, the majority has always believed that men are passive objects controlled by some superhuman or superindividual authority — and for thousands of years, people have gone hungry.

One of the oldest, if not *the* oldest, form of pagan worship is based on the idea that human destiny is controlled by the over-all will-of-the-tribe, rather than by the initiative and free will of the individual persons who make up the tribe. It is true that human beings must exchange mutual aid with each other on this inhospitable and dangerous planet. Perhaps from a dim sense of this natural kinship — the brotherhood of man — savages in prehistoric times came to believe that they were governed by the spirit of Demos, a superindividual will of the "mass," endowed with omnipotent power and authority.

The welfare of this mystic being is called "the common good," which is supposed to be more important than the good of the individual — just as the health of a human body is more important than the life of any cell in it. It is in this concept that we find the origin of human sacrifice to the pagan gods. No one hesitates to destroy the cells of the hair on his head nor of the nails on his fingers or toes. They are not important in themselves. Their only value is their use to the body as a whole. Thus, for that "common good" they are sacrificed without a moment's thought or pity.

It was precisely in that spirit that the ancient Aztec priest thrust a knife into the human victim on the altar and, with holy incantations, tore out the bleeding heart. In that same spirit, the Cretans sacrificed their loveliest daughters to the Minoan bull, and the Carthaginians burned their living babies to placate the great god, Moloch.

Some insects actually do seem to be controlled by an authority outside themselves. The honeybee, for example, appears to be wholly lacking in self-faith and individual initiative. A will-of-the-swarm seems to control it. The bee's life is exhausted in selfless, changeless toil for the common good. The swarm itself seems to be the living creature. If the queen is taken away, a hundred thousand bees die, just as a headless body dies.

Man versus Bee

The collectivists, ancient and modern, contend that human society should be set up like the beehive. In a way, it is an appealing concept — at least to the theorists, including the majority of professional writers. It is much simpler to assume that human beings "stay put" or that there should be some overriding authority that would make them stay put. But to think that way is to think like a bee — if a bee really thinks.

The plain fact of the matter is that human beings, with their hopes and aspirations and the faculty for reasoning, are very different from bees. Man combines conscious curiosity with the lessons of experience and, when permitted to do so, makes the combination pay continuous dividends. In contrast to the lower animals, he includes himself and his social affairs within the scope of his curiosity.

Bees, down through the ages, continue to act like automatons and keep on building the same little cells of wax. But human society is made up of unpredictable relationships between individual persons. It is boy meeting girl, Mrs. Jones telephoning Mrs. Smith, Robinson buying a cigar, the motorist stopping for gas, the minister making his round of calls, the postman delivering mail, the lobbyist tipping the bellboy and meeting a congressman, the school child bargaining for bubble gum, the dentist saying, "Wider, please!" Society is the innumerable relationships of persons in their infinite variety in space and in time.

The Purpose of Society

And what is the one constant element in all these relationships? Why does one person want to meet another person? What is the human purpose in society?

It is to exchange one good for another good more desired. Putting it on a personal basis, it is a matter of benefiting yourself by getting something you desire from another person who, at the same time, benefits himself by getting something that he desires from you. The object of such contacts is the peaceful exchange of benefits, mutual aid, co-operation — for each person's gain. The incalculable sum of all these meetings is human society, which is simply all the individual human actions that express the brotherhood of man.

To discuss the welfare and responsibilities of society as an abstract whole, as if it were like a bee swarm, is an oversimplification and a fantasy. The real human world is made by persons, not by societies. The only human development is the self-development of the individual person. There is no short cut!

But even today, many civilized persons — nice people, cultured, gentle, and kind, our friends and our neighbors, almost all of us at some time or another — have harbored the pagan belief that the sacrifice of the individual person serves a higher good. The superstition lingers in the false ideal of selflessness — which emphasizes conformity to the will-of-the-mass — as against the Christian virtues of self-reliance, self-improvement, self-faith, self-respect, self-discipline, and a recognition of one's *duties* as well as one's *rights*.

Such thinking is promoted under the banner of social reform, but it gives rise to the tyrants of "do-goodism" — the führers, the dictators, the overlords — who slaughter their own subjects, the very people who look to them for the more abundant life and for protection against harm.

Today such killings are called "liquidation," "blood purge," "social engineering"; but they are defended on the basis of pagan barbarism — a sacrifice of the individual under the alibi of what is claimed to be the "common good."

The Humanitarian with the Guillotine

In her discerning book, *The God of the Machine,* Isabel Paterson draws important distinctions between Christian kindliness directed toward the relief of distress, and the misguided efforts of those who would make it a vehicle for self-aggrandizement.

She points out that most of the major ills of the world have been caused by well-meaning people who ignored the principle of individual freedom, except as applied to themselves, and who were obsessed with fanatical zeal to improve the lot of mankind-in-the-mass through some pet formula of their own. "It is at this point," she says, "that the humanitarian sets up the guillotine."[1]

[1] The direct quotations and specific references used in this book are numbered consecutively and the sources are listed on page 266.

Although prompted by good intentions, such a program is usually the outgrowth of egomania fanned by self-hypnotism. As stated before, it is based on this idea: "I am right. Those who disagree are wrong. If they can't be forced into line, they must be destroyed."

Egoism, a natural human trait, is constructive when kept within bounds. But it is highly presumptuous of any mortal man to assume that he is endowed with such fantastic ability that he can run the affairs of all his fellow-men better than they, as individuals, can run their own personal affairs.

As Miss Paterson observes, the harm done by ordinary criminals, murderers, gangsters, and thieves is negligible in comparison with the agony inflicted upon human beings by the professional "do-gooders," who attempt to set themselves up as gods on earth and who would ruthlessly force their views on all others — with the abiding assurance that the end justifies the means.

But it is a mistake to assume that the do-gooders are insincere. The danger lies in the fact that their faith is just as devout and just as ardent as that of the ancient Aztec priest.

Chapter 5

SOCIALISM AND/OR COMMUNISM

The nearest approach to the bee swarm is found in socialism or communism — whichever term you care to use. There is not much choice between the two; they both aim at world collectivism. The only difference is a variation of viewpoint as to what tactics and procedures should be used to bring it about.

Up to 1917, the words *socialism* and *communism* were used as synonymous and interchangeable terms. But incident to the Russian Revolution, they began to be used to distinguish between the Second International and the Third International.

Perhaps we had better go back a little and briefly review the events that led to the present-day confusion. In the middle of the 19th century, a German named Karl Heinrich Marx, with the support of the wealthy Friedrich Engels, presented the ancient will-of-the-swarm superstition in modern dress, embellished with pseudo-scientific theories. His voluminous writings include *The Communist Manifesto* (1848) and *Das Kapital* (1867).

This was during the period when the so-called Industrial Revolution was just beginning to make headway in lifting the burden of heavy labor from the back of mankind. But Marx misinterpreted the trend. He mistook the new tools of freedom as being tools of further oppression.

He contended that capitalism, under the Machine Age, would devour an increasing share of the wealth and that the workingman would be reduced to pitiable destitution unless all the peoples of the world could be organized on a uniform, socialistic basis.

Frederic Bastiat

It is interesting to note that in the early 1840's, a brilliant young French economist, Frederic Bastiat, had reached the opposite conclusion. He said:

"In proportion as capital is accumulated, the *absolute share* of the total production going to the capitalist increases, and the *proportional share* going to the capitalist *decreases;* both the absolute and proportional share of the total production going to the laborer *increases.* The reverse of this happens when capital is decreased."

Here are some hypothetical figures to illustrate Bastiat's theory. The figures are used merely to *indicate the direction* of a relationship that occurs when capital accumulation increases:

	Units	To owners	To employees
When total national product is	50	10	40
" " " product is	75	12	63
" " " product is	100	14	86

The trend Bastiat predicted in the division of the national product is just what happened under increased capital formation in the free market of the U.S.A.*

But Marx and his followers were laboring under the Old World delusion of a static economy. It was inconceivable to them that changes in the techniques of production would bring far-reaching changes in other directions.

They believed industrial capitalism to be the natural forerunner of socialism; that to bring about the world millenium they must concentrate, first of all, on highly developed capitalistic countries — using the processes of attrition, boring from within, fomenting dissension and class hatred, and promoting collectivist measures through existing governmental agencies. This is something like jujitsu, which has been described as the technique of de-

---

* The story of Frederic Bastiat is much in contrast to that of Karl Marx. Bastiat earned his own living and paid his own way. He was a brilliant writer, and his articles found a ready market. Just as the American revolutionists were the first to accept the Christian principle of man's natural freedom as the foundation of a political structure, Bastiat was the first to apply the principle to economic analysis.

In contrast to Marx and Engels, he never forgot the spirit and soul of man; and, with hammer-blow logic brightened by a high sense of humor, he drove home the doctrine of liberation and attainment through individual effort. But Bastiat was no match for the highly organized proponents of class hatred, and he was defeated at the polls in 1848. Exhausted by overwork and robbed of his voice by tuberculosis, he continued to fight until his death in 1850, at the age of forty-nine.

Frederic Bastiat might be described as "the Tom Paine of economics." To date, he has no successor; and the carrying on of his work should be a challenge to some freedom-loving American of the younger generation.

English translations of three of his brilliant and scintillating books are now available: Social Fallacies and Harmonies of Political Economy (Santa Ana, Calif.: Register Publishing Co., Ltd., 1944); The Law (Irvington-on-Hudson, N. Y.: Foundation for Economic Education, 1950).

feating an opponent by turning his own strength against him.

In other words, it was a program of inducing capitalism to commit suicide, then stepping in and taking things over. The First International and the Second International Socialist parties were operated from that viewpoint.

Lenin

But at a London conference in 1903, just 20 years after the death of Marx, a young Russian named Vladimir Ilich Ulianov, who later became known as Lenin, split the Russian section of the Second International on a question of tactics. The process of obtaining power through political maneuvers and infiltration was too slow for him. Lenin insisted that, in the case of Russia, his professional terrorists could take over the government by force without waiting for that country to pass through the stage of modern capitalism.

Lenin and his followers set themselves up as the Third International, which came to be known as the Communist party. The shattered fragments of the Second International, including the British Labour party, continue to call themselves Socialists.

But there is really no distinction between the Socialists and the Communists, except from the standpoint of tactics in getting started; and that difference is less clearly defined than formerly because, outside of Russia, the Third International uses either force or intrigue, or a combination of the two—whichever seems propitious.

Socialism and communism, in fact all forms of collectivism, rest on the same will-of-the-swarm idea: The *in-*

dividual is nothing; the strength of the *party* is the only thing that matters!

Plutarch's account of ancient Sparta (600 B.C.) is an apt description of communism as it is practiced today:

"Their discipline continued still after they were full-grown men. No one was allowed to live after his own fancy; but the city was a sort of [military] camp, in which every man had his share of provisions and business set out. . . . [Lycurgus] bred up his citizens in such a way that they neither would nor could live by themselves; they were to make themselves one with the public good, and, clustering like bees around their commander, be by their zeal and public spirit carried all but out of themselves."[2]

The phrase "all but" is the obstinate difference between a man and a bee.

For a hundred years or more, the Spartans lived their Spartan lives in changeless routine. When King Agis IV tried to raise their standard of living, they killed him. Finally, their less communistic neighbors defeated them in war and ended the commune.

But the idea of the bee swarm still persists.

Law of Lek

After a visit to the Dinaric Alps in the 1920's, Rose Wilder Lane reports:

"The Dukhagini in the Dinaric Alps were living in the same obedience to their Law of Lek. I tried for hours to convince some of them that a man can own a house.

"A dangerously radical woman of the village was demanding a house. She had helped her husband build it; now she was a childless widow, but she wanted to keep that house. It was an ordinary house; a small, stone-walled, stone-roofed hovel, without floor, window, or chimney.

"Obstinately anti-social, she doggedly repeated, 'With these hands, my hands, I built up the walls. I laid the roof-stones with my hands. It is my house. I want my house.'

"The villagers said, 'It is a madness. A spirit of the rocks, not human, has entered into her.'

"They were intelligent. My plea for the woman astounded them, but upon reflection they produced most of the sound arguments for communism: economic equality, economic security, social order.

"I said that in America a man owns a house. They could not believe it; they admired America. They had heard of its marvels; during the recent world war they had seen with their eyes the airplanes from that fabulous land.

Taxes

"They questioned me shrewdly. I staggered myself by mentioning taxes; I had to admit that an American pays the tribe for possession of a house. This seemed to concede that the American tribe does own the house. I was routed; their high opinion of my country was restored.

"They were unable to imagine that any security, order, or justice could exist among men who were not controlled by some intangible Authority, which could not permit an individual to own a house."[3]

Collectivism versus Freedom

The practice of communism has not been confined to the Old World. The North American mound builders were probably communistic — certainly the American Indians were, and the Pilgrim Fathers established communism on the *Mayflower* and attempted to operate Plymouth as a commune.

But they found themselves up against the stern realities of a frontier wilderness. Their theories were overshadowed by the facts of the situation. Their lives depended on applying their individual energies to the providing of food and shelter. Half of them starved during the first winter, and the necessity for survival forced them to break up the commune and put each person on his own. They learned an important lesson; and from then on, they prospered.

But in later years, after the United States was formed, Americans and Europeans eagerly established communistic settlements from coast to coast.*

*Examples are: Hancock, Harvard, Shirley, Tyringham in Massachusetts; Alfred and New Gloucester in Maine; Mount Lebanon, Watervliet, Groveland, Oneida (yes, Community Silver) in New York; South Union and Pleasant Hill in Kentucky; Bethlehem and Economy in Pennsylvania; Union Village, North Union, Watervliet, Whitewater, Zoar in Ohio; Wallingford and Enfield in Connecticut; Bishop Hill, Illinois; Amana, Iowa; Corning and Bethel in Missouri; Cedarvale, Kansas; Aurora, Oregon. In the flowering of New England, Emerson's friends created the communist blossom, Brook Farm. Mr. Upton Sinclair, recently an almost-successful candidate for governor of California, began his fight for a glorious new future by founding the short-lived commune, Helicon Home Colony in New Jersey.

One after another, these experiments have failed, despite the fact that they were close-knit communities made up of fervent volunteers who, generally speaking, were bound together by a common religious faith. The founders died off. The younger generation couldn't help but notice what was going on in surrounding communities. The result was discontent and dissension. When a communistic community is set up alongside a community with a free economy, the contrast is too great to be ignored.

Regardless of the theory of the thing, human energies simply do not function in the manner of the bee swarm, and any attempt to govern the actions of multitudes of men always results in oppressive power being placed in the hands of the few.

Under communism, everything is run by the "masses." At least, that's the theory of the thing. But in actual practice, it doesn't work out that way. There must be some strong person or small group of persons to sit in the saddle and eliminate any ideas that are opposed to the so-called common good — as determined by the strong person or small group of persons.

Thus, in order to put the theories into practice, it is admittedly necessary to employ methods that are diametrically opposed to what communism is supposed to represent; and the necessity becomes increasingly obvious when the attempt is made to extend communism over a wide area.

In line with the teachings of Marx, the proponents admit the necessity but argue that it is merely a temporary measure — that the dictatorship will automatically "wither away" just as soon as things get going. They contend that history decrees this withering away, but the facts do not bear out the theory. In all history, there is no evidence of any dictatorship ever withering away. Dictatorship always feeds on itself. The ruthless tactics necessary to get it started become increasingly ruthless in the efforts to conceal the errors and defects of a scheme that can't be made to work.

Inevitable Result

Human energy and individual initiative are put in a strait jacket, and the inevitable result is poverty and distress leading into war. It may be internal rebellion, or it may be war of aggression against other people. Those in power naturally prefer the latter course. It provides the opportunity to draw attention away from failures at home, with the alluring possibility of taking wealth from others — and getting away with it.

Since the aim of communism is economic equality and security, those in charge must, in line with the practice of Lycurgus, set things up as a military camp — every man having his share of provisions and his business laid out for him. Thereafter, no person can be permitted to live and work "after his own fancy" because that would not be communism.

If some individual, on his own initiative, tries to act in a new way, to change living conditions — if, like King Agis IV, he tries to introduce money or, like the woman in the Dukhagin, to have a whole hovel for himself when the commune is not planned on such a high economic level; or if, as happened in Amana, Iowa in 1900, he wants to invent a motorcar — he has to get the consent of his comrades. And the chances are that they will not give their consent. To let him have his way would endanger the faith that keeps the commune in existence.

Artificial Respiration

In establishing a communistic state, it is possible to take advantage of everything that has gone before and to borrow techniques and ideas from other countries. It is also possible to set up and maintain bureaus of scientists, research workers, and inventors, under the control of the state.

But even under such a policy, the communistic state will lag behind those countries in which the opportunity for free initiative extends to the entire population instead of to a chosen few.

It was the goal of the Soviet dictators to industrialize Russia by raising its production to the American level of 1917. The program has continually lagged behind expectations, despite the fact that it has been greatly aided by materials, techniques, and personal services furnished by American industrialists and engineers.

Communism, regardless of the trimmings, is an attempt to make a static world in a dynamic and changing universe. To whatever degree it succeeds partially — for a length of time — it will be at the expense of progress. The scale of living will tend to remain at the same or a lower level than when the commune was first established.

There is abundant historical evidence in support of that statement; underlying such evidence is the indisputable fact that nothing but new and better ways of using human energy can raise a scale of living. And since human energy is generated and controlled by individual persons, any new way of using it must come from the efforts of an individual person to make something that does not now exist. (In a later chapter, this will be discussed in considerable detail.)

Fact and Fallacy

In all fairness, it must be said that communism recognizes human equality and the brotherhood of man — in theory at least. But it fails to recognize the *real nature* of man.

The Communist has not yet seen the fallacy in the ancient, infantile assumption that individual persons are controlled by some superindividual authority. He does not question this pagan superstition. He takes it for granted. To him, individuals are merely cells of a larger organism — the tribe, the people, society, the mass. Spartans called it *Sparta;* the villagers of Dukhagin called it the *Law of Lek;* Hegel and Treitschke called it *the State;* Karl Marx called it *Economic Necessity;* Lenin called it the *Dictatorship of the Proletariat;* Mussolini called it *Immortal Italy;* Hitler, *the German Race.*

But regardless of what it may be called, it is the self-surrender of the individual to the will of pagan authority, which the collectivists believe to be "the common good." And so, with a fanatic zeal and a deep-seated conviction that the end justifies the means, they revert to pre-Christian savagery and revive the practice of human sacrifice in order to purge or cleanse society of all persons, classes, and races that do not share their views.

There is some refuge from certain other forms of

[52]

tyranny. Generally speaking, these are less thoroughly organized and not so remorselessly armed with the self-righteousness of the "humanitarian with the guillotine." But the misguided benevolence of complete social and economic power always leads to ruthless suppression of religious freedom, personal freedom, freedom of expression, and even freedom of thought.

Chapter 6

THE LIVING AUTHORITIES

The pagan may lose confidence in one particular kind of authority. When his faith begins to waver, he is more likely to change the name of the imaginary authority — or to assume that it controls everyone except himself — than to accept the nonpagan view that human beings are self-controlling. Old World minds have rarely doubted that they are controlled by some authority outside themselves; but down through the ages, they have become inclined to the belief that the authority resides in a human form — either a living god or some exalted person who, by reason of birth, ancestry, class, race, or color, is endowed with divine or supernatural attributes which make him the living embodiment of God.

The pharaohs of Egypt, the Roman emperors, and the Japanese mikados were believed to be gods in human form. Until 1911, the empress of China was a sacred being. The Tibetans still believe that God is incarnate in their Grand Lama. In 1776, Continental Europeans, South and Central Americans, and most North Americans believed that their kings were God's appointed agents, ruling by divine right. As recently as the first World War, most Europeans and all Asiatics took it for granted that anyone of royal blood was endowed with divine qualities.

In all cases, such beliefs rest on the pagan superstition that the individual is not responsible for his acts; that he must depend on these superhuman persons who have both the right and the power to control the lives of people assumed to be their natural inferiors.

Whether the monarch is looked upon as a living god or as God's personal agent, all property is at his disposal; and in practice, he bestows great wealth and the exercise of some authority on a few persons, who then form a superior class — nobles, samurai, aristocrats, bureaucratic ministers in control of this, that, and the other. Such men, headed by their emperor, their king, or their queen, are looked upon as the government.

Theory versus Practice

In theory, the change from ancient communism to an "omnipotent" living authority should not make much difference in the lives of the people; but in actual practice, it usually brings certain benefits. Those who rule by "divine right" are inclined to accept their inherited authority as a matter of course. Generally speaking, they do not have the ruthless ambition of the self-made dictator who rises to power in a collectivist society. And again generally speaking, they are not so remorselessly armed with the mystical self-righteousness of the "humanitarian with the guillotine."

The superficialities of court life provide an outlet for royal energy that is less harmful, and far less expensive, than unintelligent meddling. The monarch does not live forever. He dies, and another monarch takes his place. Such interruptions, in contrast to the communistic state, are usually accompanied by changes in rules and regulations. The static routine is broken. Mystical fanaticism is reduced, and individual energy tends to assert itself to some degree.

So whenever and wherever any large number of persons has broken away from the changeless routine of ancient communism, their energies have worked a little, by fits and starts, to improve their living conditions.

For instance: During 60 centuries, human energy (already having the wheel) managed to get a cart onto two wheels and to attach knives to them in order to kill the subjects of their king's enemy-king. Then, after a lapse that almost lost the wheel, human energy finally got a cart onto four wheels. But up to the time of George Washington, all the efforts of men to improve transportation had only been able to produce a coach — and only for the very rich. Gilded and supported on leather straps above four ironshod wheels, you may see it today in the carriage house at Mount Vernon.

Another instance: Three thousand years ago in Greece, men knew the principle of the steam engine. The Greeks spread their civilization over the known world after the Macedonians conquered it. Yet today on the Tigris and the Euphrates, men are still paddling logs hollowed out by fire or are drifting downstream in bowls of rawhide stretched on saplings. And from Baghdad, they walk back upstream for a thousand miles, just as American flatboatmen in colonial times used to walk back from New Orleans to Pittsburgh.

Another instance: For 40 centuries, men sailed boats. In addition to sails, the Phoenicians used oars. The Romans went a step further, using two or three banks of oars with slaves chained to each oar. Through overseers using whips, the captain had some control of the boat's direction and speed. This questionable advance was lost, and Columbus sailed in ships dependent wholly on the winds. But by 1776, the French were again using the Roman galley system, with convicts chained to the oars.

Cause and Effect

The above are only a few examples illustrating that, under the living authorities, human energy has worked in jerks, so to speak. In any few hundred years of Old World history, we find a succession of convulsive efforts and collapses — as if a living thing were roped down and struggling.

That is precisely what was happening. Human energy could not get to work at its primary, natural job of producing and distributing the necessities of human life. Whenever men began to develop farming and crafts and trade, government stopped them.

Mind you, the government never intended to stop them; indeed, its honest aim was to help them. But the effect was the opposite, for the simple reason that efforts to help were based on the false notion that human energy and individual initiative can be directed and controlled through an overriding authority, using the brute force of military and police power.

Force and fear have their uses — we will come to that in a moment — but they are ineffective in stimulating ambition, initiative, creative effort, and perseverance. Threats of the concentration camp or the firing squad might make a man run a little faster or work a little harder — at least for a time — but fear reduces endurance and hastens fatigue. It also works at cross-purposes to mental development and moral growth. It depresses the higher nerve centers, and its continued use tends to paralyze the normal processes of thought.

Thus it is that slave labor has never been able to compete with free men in occupations requiring a high degree of initiative, resourcefulness, and persistence.

Furthermore, the unbridled use of arbitrary power, maintained through force and fear, always has a demoralizing and degenerating effect on those who use it. It breeds arrogance, intolerance, and sadism. Like the dope habit, it may start out innocently enough; but it feeds on itself, and things go from bad to worse. The more a person relies on it, the greater the temptation to increase the dose. Thus the "temporary" remedy becomes a pernicious habit, and it is almost impossible to turn back.

It is true that man has not yet attained the degree of intelligence which makes it possible to do away entirely with the use of force. When one man or a small group of men reverts to animal-like violence, decent people have only one choice: They must use force as a means of neutralizing the *misuse* of force.

Policemen are needed to deal with the occasional criminal, robber, or killer who hinders the constructive work of the majority. Where there is no police force, every man must be ready to defend himself and his property; and this takes time away from useful work.

Vigilance Committee

In the pioneer days of our own wild West, each man carried a gun. The need for force was rare, and few of them ever shot anybody. But everyone had to be armed and ready, on the off-chance that he might have to shoot it out with a "bad man."

Being normal men, they did not like to lug guns around; they wanted to get on with their natural jobs — clearing land, planting crops, raising cattle, building towns. To do their work in security and peace, they had to get rid of the outlaw. So when emergencies arose, they would organize themselves into a vigilance committee, go after the outlaw, and string him up. They did this clear across the continent, from the Yadkin to the Rio Grande, the Golden Gate, and the Columbia.

Although the vigilance committee was created by honest citizens as a means of stopping thieves and murderers, it sometimes resulted in gangsterism. The right-thinking members were inclined to drop out as soon as the emergency was over because no right-thinking person likes the idea of killing a fellow man. But the less scrupulous would stay in; and once having broken the bond of human kinship that protects men from violence against each other, some of them became killers. Thus, it frequently happened that the vigilance committee degenerated into a group of lawless gangsters, and the situation was worse than before.*

Orderly Solution

So it was only natural that peaceful men should organize a legal force to make a regular job of preserving law and order. They selected a few of their number and said to

*This same sequence of events had its parallel, on a huge and aggravated scale, in the kind of things that happened in Europe during the chaotic period between the two world wars.

them, in effect: "You keep the peace. Sheriff, you carry the gun for all of us from now on. You, Judge, call on 12 of us to decide what to do with any 'bad man' that the sheriff catches alive. It's your job to preserve law and order so that the rest of us can get our work done without interference. You give your whole time to it, and we'll supply you with food, shelter, and other necessities."

That is a good example of government stripped to its bare essentials. It is a justifiable use of force because it increases the general well-being and the productive output of normal citizens by enabling them to use their energies to the best advantage, without interference.

Moral versus Legal

Human energy cannot operate effectively except when men are free to act and to be responsible for their actions. But liberty does not mean license; for no one has a right to infringe upon the rights of others. Certain restraints are necessary, and they are provided in two ways:

1. *Legal restraints* — the passing of laws to be administered by governmental agencies and enforced by police power.
2. *Moral restraints* — which depend on individual self-discipline, logical reasoning, good sportsmanship, and a consideration for the rights of others.

Legal restraints, as already pointed out, are useful in curbing activities which are clearly injurious and which are generally recognized as being opposed to the best interests of all decent people. But legal restraints are inadequate when we get over into the area of question-able practices which cannot be sharply defined, or which are not easily detected, or which are not generally dis-approved.

It's easy to say "Let's settle this or that by passing a law." But laws on the statute books can never be an ade-quate substitute for moral restraint based on enlightened self-interest — which means a recognition of one's duties as well as of one's rights.

The extension of laws into areas where they cannot be enforced does more harm than good:

1. It takes emphasis away from personal responsibility and promotes the dangerous notion that legalized force can be used as a substitute for self-control and individual morality.

2. It increases red tape and government overhead, without accomplishing the intended result.

3. It weakens respect for the really necessary laws.

4. Law observance breaks down, and remedy is sought in bolstering the penalties and in passing addi-tional laws.

5. Along with it all, the administrative and enforce-ment facilities are further increased, which means taking more and more people away from produc-tive work.

Any attempt to give to government the responsibilities which properly belong to the individual citizens works at cross-purposes to the advancement of personal free-dom. It retards progress — morally as well as along the lines of greater productivity. Look at it from any angle you please, but there's no escaping the conclusion that moral restraints are more efficient than legal restraints — which, incidentally, is just another way of saying that honesty and decency are profitable.

Right here the objection may be raised that "to depend on moral restraints calls for quite a change in human behavior." I won't attempt to argue the point — except to say that changes and further improvements in the direction of enlightened self-interest and personal responsibility are not nearly so difficult to attain as the unnatural changes that are advocated by those who would repress individual development and reduce human beings to the status of the beehive.

Progress lies in working in harmony with the fundamental nature of man, not in reverting to the pagan superstition which, for over 6,000 years, has suppressed individual initiative and kept human energy in a strait jacket.

Regimentation

In modern times, this pagan superstition is known by the persuasive name *planned economy*, which is nothing more than a weasel word for socialism or communism or fascism. Call it anything you please, but it is still the pagan concept, based on a misunderstanding of human energy. It is an attempt to make a static world in a dynamic and changing universe. It is an attempt to make the gasoline engine run on steam or the steam engine run on gasoline. In brief, it is an attempt to do the impossible.

It is difficult for Americans to understand the stagnating effects of regimentation and how it leads to greater and greater oppressions. It is generally outside the range of our experience because we have lived in a new kind of world where human energy and initiative have usually worked under the natural control of the individual— which is the only way that they can ever work effectively.

For 160 years, during the greatest demonstration of progress that the world has ever known, each American has been mostly free to decide for himself how to earn money and whether to save or spend it; whether to go to school or go to work; whether to stick to his job or leave it and get another—or go into business on his own; whether to plant cotton or corn; whether to rent or buy or build a house; how much he would, or would not, pay for a shirt or a car; and what he would take for the Jersey calf or the old jalopy.

Chapter 7

THE STATIC CENTER

THERE is no denying the fact that human beings progress and prosper in proportion to the degree to which individual initiative is permitted, or at least *not* prevented. But Old World government has always been based on the fallacious idea of an authority controlling a planned economy for the so-called common good. Actually, it is nothing more than the arbitrary use of physical force by persons upon persons; and regardless of the high motives and good intentions, the effect is the same — it always slows down progress and hinders the production and distribution of the necessities of life.

This explains the historical fact — at first surprising — that a sincere, conscientious, hard-working ruler always does the most harm to his own subjects. The lazy, dissolute ruler neglects his job. Caligula, for instance, merely wasted goods in riotous extravagance and tortured just a few hundred of his subjects for his personal enjoyment. The majority of the people always get along comparatively well under a ruler like Caligula.

It was the sober, ascetic, industrious Augustus Caesar, toiling for the welfare of his Empire and its people, who began the destruction of Rome and laid the foundation for the misery and human degradation which Europeans suffered for centuries thereafter. He launched a planned economy which was to serve as the basis for the Roman world peace. The Roman legions gave it to all the people of the then-known world — as fast as they could be conquered. From Africa and Asia to England that peace extended, and it was designed to last forever.

The hairsplitting economic regulations were perfected by Diocletian, whose stern directives were so efficiently administered that farmers could no longer farm; and many of the small businessmen, faced with starvation, committed suicide in preference to being executed for black marketing.

There was no work for the workingman, so the beneficent government stepped in and, by taxing the rich, managed for a while to provide the populace with bread and circus tickets.

But that was no solution. The improvement was short-lived. Money can't buy goods unless the goods are produced.

The mounting taxes put more and more people out of business. An increasing number of workers were forced onto tax-supported relief until there was not enough productive energy at work to pay the tax bills. The great Roman Empire — with its plans for a thousand years of peace and security — collapsed into the Dark Ages.

That was the work of the *best* of emperors.

British Empire

At the other extreme, let us turn to England, which, for many centuries, was blessed with some of the worst rulers ever to wear a crown. If Richard the Lion-Hearted had stayed at home and tended to his job, or if King John had been half as good a ruler as his grandfather, there never would have been a Magna Charta for freedom.

The only able Tudor was Queen Elizabeth, whose father, Henry VIII, had left England so uncontrolled that it took all her energy and wit just to hold on to her throne. There was no time left for her to rule, and never was a realm so loosely governed. She built up the British Navy by doing nothing for it. She told her sea captains to act on their own responsibility and at their own expense. She wouldn't even pay for the powder and lead they used in defending England against the Spanish Armada. Her plan was to do *no* planning. With great firmness of character and consistency of purpose, she always decided to decide nothing. By this highly intelligent means, she let her subjects found the British Empire.

The good Queen Bess was succeeded by the Stuarts — a charming, self-indulgent breed of "divine right" kings, the poodle dogs of their species, with not a moral under their curly wigs. They governed so negligently that the butchers and bakers and candlestick makers chucked them off the throne and made ex-brewer Cromwell the ruler of England.

Even after such a lesson, the Stuarts later came back to power so lazily that Charles II gave his parliament the order: "I pray, contrive any good short bills which may improve the industry of the nation."[4]

That was all. And while the King uttered such idle words, his police were so few that it was no longer necessary to bribe them. Thousands of smugglers took over, and boomed British foreign trade from every port and cove. They were so numerous that a wit described "Merrie England" as a piece of land entirely surrounded by smugglers!

Woolen Shrouds

At that time, Continental weavers depended on England for raw wool, which they wove into cloth far superior to the product of English looms. To protect the domestic manufacturers, Parliament prohibited any further export of English wool. Of course, this measure would have ruined the English woolgrowers; but as always in all history, realistic tradesmen rescued commerce.

And when the prospering English woolgrowers expanded production so rapidly that the black marketeers could no longer handle all the export trade, Charles offered only one little remedy for "overproduction." He decreed that in England no corpse could be buried that was not wrapped in a woolen shroud of domestic manufacture.

The measure was strictly enforced; the wool was buried, but ghouls dug up the corpses and stole the shrouds, which, through bootlegging, finally covered the naked legs of London's workingmen.

Germany and France

The Continental rulers with their powerful police forces were more efficient, especially in the Germanies where everything was so thoroughly regulated that production and commerce almost ceased to exist. And here is Buckle's comment, with particular reference to France:

"In every quarter, and at every moment, the hand of government was felt. Duties on importation, and duties on exportation; bounties to raise up a losing trade, and taxes to pull down a remunerative one; this branch of industry forbidden, and that branch of industry encouraged; one article of commerce must not be grown, because it was grown in the colonies, another article might be grown and bought, but not sold again, while a third article might be bought and sold, but not leave the country. Then, too, we find laws to regulate wages; laws to regulate prices; laws to regulate profits; laws to regulate the interest of money; custom-house arrangements of the most vexatious kind, aided by a complicated scheme, which was well called the sliding scale, — a scheme of such perverse ingenuity, that the duties constantly varied on the same article, and no man could calculate beforehand what he would have to pay. . . . The tolls were so onerous, as to double and often quadruple the cost of production. . . . A large part of all this was by way of protection: that is to say, the money was avowedly raised, and the inconvenience suffered, not for the use of the government, but for the benefit of the people; in other words, the industrious classes were robbed, in order that industry might thrive.

". . . the first inevitable consequence was, that, in every part of Europe, there arose numerous and powerful gangs of armed smugglers, who lived by disobeying the laws which their ignorant rulers had imposed. These men, desperate from fear of punishment . . . spread, wherever they came, drunkenness, theft, and dissoluteness; and familiarized their associates with those coarse and swinish debaucheries, which were the natural habits of so vagrant and lawless a life."[5]

Indeed, nothing but smuggling kept the French from

starving to death under the care of their state, benevolently planned for their welfare.

During the reign of Louis XIV, the French weavers went through a whole season without moving a shuttle. While the people were waiting for clothes, the weavers were waiting for the government to tell them what kind of cloth they would be allowed to weave, what color it should be, and how many threads would be permitted for each inch of warp and woof.

The regulations on the textile industry alone covered over 3,000 pages, and they were different for each district. The manufacturers of Saint-Maixent, for example, had to negotiate for four years before the government allowed them to use black warp, and they never did get permission to use black woof.

Human energy simply does not work the way the despots and dictators would like to have it work. It works only under its natural control. Any attempt to make it work through the use of police force has always failed and has held back civilization.

Weak Alibi

It is contended by some that the people of the Old World are more interested in the higher things of life, that they have never had any desire for what is scornfully called the "material civilization" of the Western world.

Perhaps. And perhaps slaves carrying loads on their backs were not permitted to invent a four-wheeled wagon. It's hard to say. But surely, human beings — all human beings — have always wanted food. Yet for 6,000 years, they have been hungry and dying of hunger. Under such conditions, there is not much chance for widespread improvement along cultural and moral lines. (This will be dealt with more fully in a later chapter.)

Egyptians erected their stately pyramids — and sold their daughters to brothels because they could not feed them. Athenians built their proud Parthenon and went to their democratic elections — while desolate wails came from pottery jars along their streets, where babies were dying. A mother's friends would put her baby into a jar to die slowly, in the forlorn hope that it might be rescued by someone who could afford to feed a child.

Perpetual Famines

In Asia and Africa famines have never ceased. In Europe, the working people have never yet obtained enough milk, butter, fruit. Over the greater part of this earth, women as well as men continue to give 16 hours of literally killing labor for the day's meager food. In peaceful Shanghai's most prosperous days, every morning at dawn the policemen gathered up from the streets the bodies of the men, women, and children who had died of hunger during the night. It was a routine job!

So much for progress during the past 6,000 years. But why consider such a short period?

As far back as 250,000 years ago, people lived in caves in France and Spain. People still live in caves in France and Spain. The cliffs of Chinchilla are still inhabited. At Coria, the pottery workers live as they have always lived — along the banks of the Guadalquivir, in holes without floors or windows. In Italy, in Greece, in Yugoslavia, in Russia, many people still live underground.

Ancestral Habitat

Mrs. Lane writes:

"When American Red Cross workers went into the Balkans after the first World War, they found families living in a clay bank at Montenegro's largest city. They were horrified. So was I. I wrote a piece about those homeless victims of war that should have wrung dollars from the stoniest American pocketbook. Only, before I finished it, I went back with an interpreter to give some first aid to those miserable refugees. My sympathetic questions bewildered them. They were living as they always had lived, in their ancestral homes."[8-a]

If men and women do not want to live like that — if they do not want to be always in destitution, always on the verge of starvation — they must come to realize that they, and they alone, can control their human energies.

The state is called the government, but it cannot actually govern the individual acts of any person because of the nature of human energy. Men in public office are only men, and no man can control another's thoughts, speech, or creative actions. No possible use of physical force can compel anyone to think, speak, or act. It can only limit, hinder, and prevent.

In the last analysis, and stripped of all the furbelows, government is nothing more than a legal monopoly of the use of physical force — by persons upon persons. And the monopoly is permitted by common consent. No government can exist without the consent and economic support of the people.

This important fact is quite obvious when you consider the frontier sheriff who was elected to protect the good men against the "bad man." It is somewhat less obvious in the case of the Old World tyrants and dictators, but the fact remains that their power rests on the consent and support of the people. The best evidence of this is that the pages of history are full of rebellions against earthly rulers.

Revolts versus Revolutions

All men who have ever obeyed a living authority have in time revolted against it. Look at the history of Assyria, Persia, Egypt, Rome, Spain, France, England; look at any record of any people living anywhere at any time in the Old World's history. Sooner or later, they revolted.

But with minor exceptions, such revolts have been directed against a *particular* authority, without disturbing the pagan belief that *some* authority should control their lives and be responsible for their welfare.

When such people do not get enough to eat, they merely conclude that the existing authority does not control them properly; that everything would be all right if they were governed by a new authority, or a stronger and wiser authority — one which would really make good on the age-old and alluring promise of "something for nothing."

So they rebel against their king and set up another king. At a later date, they rebel against him and set up still another. Then as time goes on, they rebel against monarchy itself and set up some other kind of authority. Every imaginable kind of living authority has been tried, also every possible combination — the priest and the king, the king who is the priest, the king who is a god, the king and a senate, the king and the senate and a majority, the senate and a tyrant, the tyrant and the aristocrats. Think of any combination that comes to mind. Somewhere it has been tried. Somewhere on this earth, most of them are being tried right today.

Down through the ages, century after century, time and time again, men have killed their rulers and have slaughtered one another in untold millions, in the effort to find an authority that would improve their conditions. Such rebellions sometimes bring temporary benefits. They interrupt the mechanism of attempted control and permit human energy to work a little — for a little while.

In a Circle

But the Old World revolutions are not real revolutions. They are revolutions only in the sense of a wheel rotating around a motionless center. Under the pagan view, the standard pattern has always been to overthrow one form of authority merely to replace it with another form of authority — from priest to king, from king to oligarchy, from oligarchy to despot, from despot to majority, from majority to bureaucracy, from bureaucracy to dictator, from dictator to king, from king to . . . and so on, and so on. There have been 6,000 years of it; and for 6,000 years, people have gone hungry. The simple reason is that human energy cannot be made to work efficiently except in an atmosphere of individual freedom and voluntary co-operation, based on enlightened self-interest and moral responsibility.

For Human Freedom

There has never been but one real revolution. It is the revolution against pagan fatalism — the revolution for *human freedom*.

Part III

THE REVOLUTION

Chapter 8

THE FIRST ATTEMPT

No one knows who first made the discovery that men are free. The fragmentary records begin with one person. There is no historical proof that he really existed, but the story holds its own self-evident truth; and for countless generations, it was handed down from father to son.

They said that when Ur was the great empire (about 4,000 years ago), a shepherd named Terah, accompanied by his son, his daughter-in-law, and his orphaned grandson, traveled with his flocks toward the Far West. When Terah died, the family — now headed by Abraham — continued westward. They also were shepherds, always moving with their flocks.*

That was back in the days when people believed that everything was controlled by the whims and fancies of pagan gods. Water-gods, when they felt so disposed, made water flow; sea-gods moved the waves and tides; air-gods controlled the winds; gods whispered in trees, roared in thunder, and brought rain to the fields. Fertility-gods caused seeds to sprout and women to bear children. Gods controlled men just as they controlled all other things. As water ran and winds blew, so men thought and felt and acted as the gods might will.

*All biblical references and quotations in *Mainspring* are from the King James Version.

But Abraham denied the existence of all these pagan gods. He insisted that there is only one God — the God of all things, the God who creates and judges. He taught his increasing family that God is Rightness, Reality, and Truth; that man is free and self-controlling and responsible for his own acts; that each person is free to do good or evil, as he may choose, but that any wrong act will result in punishment to the evildoer.

Incidentally, I cannot see that it is any sacrilege to observe in passing that Abraham's theological concept laid the foundation for scientific progress. So long as men labored under the delusion that the universe is controlled by the whims and fancies of prankish gods, there was no point in trying to improve anything through individual effort. Progress did not come until men began to realize that everything works according to a divine plan, the essence of which is truth and rightness.

As will be discussed in a later chapter, this applies not only to questions of morality, but also to all other things. Every engineer, every scientist, every farmer, and every mechanic knows that nothing will work, that no act will succeed, unless it is in harmony with rightness — the true nature of things as they are.

Joseph

When Abraham died, a very old man, his sons buried him in the land that is now Turkey. The record says that many years later, during one of the famines, the descendants of Abraham moved into Egypt in search of food. There, as time went on, they became rich and privileged. It seems that they had "pull" with a kinsman named Joseph, who understood the crop cycle and made himself Pharaoh's favorite by laying out a planned economy known as the "ever-normal granary."

But when the crops failed and famine came, the farmers and herdsmen had to sign away their fields and pastures in order to get back enough grain to keep from starving. Thus rank-and-file Egyptians were reduced to virtual slavery. But the privileged class, rich and secure, had no particular objection to slavery. It didn't hurt them — or at least, so they thought.

Abraham's descendants, as members of the favored class, grew and prospered and "multiplied exceedingly" — for a while. Then the old, old, endless repetition occurred once more. A new man came into power. He was anxious to gain favor with the Egyptians, and he said unto them: "Behold, the people of Israel are more and mightier than we: Come on, let us deal wisely with them."

The oppressed classes rallied to his call. They seized the Israelites' property and set about liquidating them. They placed them in bondage, worked many of them to death, and killed their babies.

Moses

Finally, a man named Moses came to the rescue. With great difficulty, he got the children of Israel out of Egypt and across the Red Sea. Some of them died on the journey, and those who came through alive were not very appreciative. After long years of slavery, they had forgotten the teachings of Abraham and expected others to take care of all their needs. They would do nothing for themselves, and soon they turned against Moses, blaming him for all their troubles. When food was scarce, they howled that he was starving them. When he didn't bring them water, they wailed that he was killing them with thirst.

One wonders how Moses stuck it out. But for 40 years, he kept on telling them that they were free men; that they were responsible for themselves. "Your murmurings *are* not against us," he told them, "but against the LORD."

But slaves are passive. They submit. They obey. And they expect to be fed.

They wanted Moses to be their king so that they could hold him responsible and blame him for everything. But Moses turned them down and kept on insisting that they were free, responsible for themselves; that there was no pagan god to control them and be responsible for them; that no man could rule another man. But the children of Israel kept on murmuring, drifting back into idolatry, and sneaking every chance to worship their pagan gods.

The Ten Commandments

Finally, as a last resort, Moses reduced the teachings of Abraham to a written code of moral law. Known as the "Ten Commandments," it stands today as the first and greatest document of individual freedom in the recorded history of man. Each of the Ten Commandments is addressed to the individual as a self-controlling person responsible for his own thoughts, words, and acts. And each of them recognizes liberty and freedom as inherent in the nature of man.

The first commandment tells the individual to reject

pagan gods and recognize his own worth as a human being, subject to no power but that of the Creator and Judge.

The second tells the individual to form no image of abstract rightness, but to direct his reverence toward the divine in truth.

The third tells the individual not to speak frivolously of the Creator and Judge. Knowledge of fundamental truth — cause and effect — is of first importance and should be taken very seriously.

The fourth tells the individual to devote some time (one day out of seven) to reflection on the eternal verities.

The fifth recognizes the family as the primary human relationship and establishes the parent's authority over the child as the only authority which a child should accept for his own profit.

The sixth stresses the sanctity of human life — the individual's right to live, which is a right that must not be violated by any other person.

The seventh establishes the principle of contract — the inviolability of promises given by persons to each other and the double sanctity of the marriage contract, which is the basis of the family.

The eighth recognizes the individual's right to own property.

The ninth recognizes free speech — the individual's control over his own utterances and his responsibility for their truth.

The tenth emphasizes again the right of ownership. Not even in thought should a person violate the property rights of another.

The Decalogue of Moses is one of the most amazing statements of truth ever written, but it was too revolutionary to find acceptance in the pagan world of his time; the ancient Israelites wanted a king rather than a code of personal conduct.

Gideon and Samuel

As time went on, they put their proposition up to Gideon. After he had freed them from the Midianites, the men of Israel said to Gideon: "Rule thou over us, both thou, and thy son, and thy son's son also: for thou hast delivered us from the hand of Midian."

Anyone who believes that government has real power will accept such an offer — either because he selfishly wants power or because, in imagined unselfishness, he wants to force others to do what he believes will be good for them.

But Gideon replied: "I will not rule over you, neither shall my son rule over you: The Lord shall rule over you."

Still the Israelites were not satisfied. They kept on trying to escape from freedom and from the responsibility that *is* freedom.

A hundred years later, their grandsons were still seeking a king. They begged the wise man Samuel to give them a king; but Samuel agreed with his precedessors and, in no uncertain terms, pointed out the fallacy of their reasoning:

"This will be the manner of the king that shall reign over you: He will take your sons, and appoint them for himself, for his chariots, and to be his horsemen; and some shall run before his chariots. And he will

[82]

appoint him captains over thousands, and captains over fifties; and will set them to ear his ground, and to reap his harvest, and to make his instruments of war. . . . And he will take your fields, and your vineyards, and your olive yards, even the best of them, and give them to his servants. And he will take the tenth of your seed, and of your vineyards. . . . And he will take your men servants, and your maid servants, and your goodliest young men . . . and put them to his work. . . . And ye shall cry out in that day because of your king which ye shall have chosen you."

That is a precise statement of the sources of a state's power and of the results of a state's attempt to control its subjects in either ancient or modern times — first the taking away of productive energy, then the rise of bureaucracy and heavy taxation, followed by stagnation and poverty, leading to ultimate destruction in war.

Samuel stated it better than I can; but the Israelites were still not convinced, and they answered: "Nay; but we will have a king over us; That we also may be like all the nations; and that our king may . . . go out before us, and fight our battles."

History Repeats

In the end, the Israelites had their way. They went back to pagan submission to an imaginary authority. They got themselves a king, in fact, a whole series of kings — including Solomon, who lived in great splendor in a fabulous palace, surrounded by magnificent public buildings paid for by ever-increasing taxes.

At long last, the Israelites were like other nations; and like other nations, they were defeated in war. Their great city was destroyed, and their conquerors used the then-ancient method of mass deportation — the same method that has been revived and vastly extended in recent times. Only a few Israelites were left in all Judea; and under Roman tyranny, they slavishly obeyed their overlords.

But the teachings of Abraham, Moses, Gideon, and Samuel had not been in vain. It is one of the greatest achievements of history that the straggling little tribes of Israelites preserved the teachings of their prophets and passed them down through countless generations.

Most of the Old World rulers have always hated the Jews. For 4,000 years, the word *Jew* has symbolized freedom and individual initiative, in contrast to the pagan concept of a static world and submission to the gods of superstition.

But the knowledge that men are free is not enough. If the human race is to progress, individual freedom must be combined and tempered with the principles of co-operation, based on a recognition of human brotherhood.

The ancient Israelites lived most of the time with no government whatever. This was not without its advantages because it permitted them to apply their full energies to raising their crops, caring for their flocks, and making their simple clothing and shelter.

But unrestrained anarchy cannot produce a well-rounded civilization. The development of production and the building of extensive commerce require organization. Effective organization depends on co-operation, and co-operation rests on a knowledge and acceptance of human brotherhood.

The New Commandment

Christ came upon the earth 2,000 years after the time of Abraham. He reiterated and crystallized the teachings of the Hebrew prophets. He spoke of the God of Abraham, the God of Truth, the God of Rightness — the God who does not control any man, but who judges the acts of every man.

Christ illustrated His teachings with practical examples — simple parables and stories expressed in terms of personal relations between individuals. Most important of all, He brought a new commandment which is the foundation of intelligent self-interest and practical cooperation: "Love thy neighbor as thyself." "Whatsoever ye would that men should do to you, do ye even so to them." "Inasmuch as ye have done *it* unto one of the least of these my brethren, ye have done *it* unto me."

Although gentle and kindly, Christ was a fighter who brought a sword of truth to destroy the pagan kingdoms. He rendered unto Caesar the things that were Caesar's, but only the things that force could take — a coin, a material thing, even life itself — never freedom. He attacked the priests. He scorned their assumption of authority and openly defied them. In sermons and parables and acts Christ always asserted individual freedom: "The kingdom of God is within you." "Our Father which art in heaven. . . . Thy kingdom come . . . in earth. . . . For thine is the kingdom. . . ." "The meek . . . shall inherit the earth."

Although He was followed by multitudes, there were few who understood the full import of His teachings. Most of them believed that they had found a leader who would set up the kind of kingdom they had urged upon Moses, Gideon, and Samuel. The time was ripe for a revolt against Rome. According to the record, Christ, could have had the kingdoms of the world. Christ refused.

Chapter 9

COMPROMISE

Abraham declared that every man is a free agent, responsible only to God. Moses reduced the teachings of Abraham to a written code of moral law, directed to the individual. Christ expanded on these teachings and added a new commandment emphasizing the principle of human brotherhood.

These events marked the turning point in a world which had long been dominated by the gods of superstition — the will-of-the-swarm and the living authorities.

In relation to recorded history, Abraham, Moses, and Christ lived in ancient times; but the pagan view to which they were opposed dates back to the beginning of primitive man, which has been estimated at 500,000 years ago. So, relatively speaking, the foundations of the Hebrew-Christian religion are of modern origin.

The new teachings were too revolutionary to be accepted all at once; even down to this day, they have never been given a thorough trial. But their impact on the deep-seated superstitions was terrific; and history since the time of Christ is largely a record of conflicts and compromises between paganism and freedom.

There had been glimmerings of freedom — perhaps independently of Abraham and the Hebrew prophets — but nowhere else do we find the principles so clearly stated and emphasized as the God-given rights of the individual person.

The Greeks

In ancient Greece, for example, there had been some degree of freedom, but it was on a class basis; and even in the days of their highest culture, the Greeks continued to cherish their pagan gods.

They believed, for example, that a man loved a woman because a god had shot an arrow into his heart. The chubby little figure on our valentines of today was as real to the Greeks as electricity is to present-day Americans.

The Greeks had implicit faith in the ability of the government to take care of their needs. It seems never to have occurred to them that the individual person is self-controlling and responsible for his own acts. They labored under the delusion that their democracy was a guarantee of peace and plenty, not realizing that unrestrained majority-rule always destroys freedom, puts the minority at the mercy of the mob, and works at cross-purposes to the effective use of human energy and individual initiative.*

Paradoxically, when not kept within bounds, the democratic process has always led to the destruction of democratic ideals and has served as a springboard to dictatorship and war. The temptation to buy votes through governmental spending is too great. Prompted by political

*It seems unfortunate that so many Americans have lost sight of the fact that our government was designed, not as a democracy, but as a republic. It is interesting to note that the word *democracy* does not appear in the Declaration of Independence or in the Constitution or in the Bill of Rights; and I have been told that prior to 1913, it had never been used in any official presidential statement. Belief in the democratic process as a defense of liberty and freedom may be just as ineffective as was the faith of the French in their Maginot line. (See Chapter 15.)

ambition or by a sincere desire to do good, and usually by both, a champion of the people emerges with the age-old and appealing promise of "something for nothing" — to be financed through ever-increasing taxes. (See pages 47, 65, 83, 146, 250.) Supply and demand are thrown out of gear — the overhead goes up; the effective use of human energy goes down; the standard of living is lowered because money cannot buy wealth that is not produced. No government can support its people, for the simple reason that a government must derive its support *from* the people.

In Greece, it was the glittering Pericles who, in the role of benefactor, set up and maintained his dictatorship through increased government spending. Then, to divert attention from the impending disaster, he led his followers into the even greater disaster of war against Sparta.

It was the beginning of the end for Greece. But there had been some degree of freedom among the upper classes, and it reflected itself in their contributions to architecture, art, science, and philosophy.

The Romans

Taking advantage of what could be learned from the Greek philosophers, the methodical Romans built a political structure based on codified law. Written codes of law had been in existence prior to the Romans, and even before the time of Moses; but they were little more than expressions of savage superstition. Instead of being based on equity and justice, they were based on cruelty and revenge — "eye for eye, tooth for tooth."

[89]

In ancient Babylon, for example, if a child were killed by a falling roof stone, the builder of the house suffered the penalty of having his own child killed in a similar manner.

But the Romans, in developing their laws, got away from tribal custom and substituted logic in the place of whim and fancy. This was an important contribution. Without written law, no one knows where he stands; but if the law is to be effective over wide areas, it must be based on something more substantial than local superstition.

The far-flung Roman Empire, which included people of vastly different customs and backgrounds, would have been impossible except for the clean-cut and reasonably just code of law under which everyone knew where he stood.

By way of illustration, imagine what would happen in the field of sports — baseball, football, hockey, etc. — if everything were left to the whim and fancy of each umpire and referee. Imagine the confusion that would result if there were no definite and logical rules laid down in advance, agreed to by both sides, and equitably enforced.

The Romans had their "rules of the game"; and generally speaking, these rules were enforced to the letter — impersonally and without prejudice. But there were different laws for different classes of people, so it could hardly be said that the rules were agreed to by both sides.

Each person in each class knew where he stood in relation to the law; and in theory, the privileged class had some say as to the fairness of the law. But dictatorships were frequent, and the interpretation of the law could be changed to meet the needs of the endless emergencies — both real and fancied.

Thus, the principles of freedom were compromised with the pagan idea of authoritarian control. The Romans were never able to solve the problem of true constitutional government. But their partial recognition of human rights under law brought the problem into the open and was not without value in leading to its solution some 1,400 years later. To say the least, the experiences of the Greeks and Romans showed how *not* to do it.

As will be seen later, the political structure of the United States is radically different from that of the Greeks or the Romans. It is based on the Ten Commandments and on the teachings of Christ. Try to rewrite the Declaration of Independence without reference to the Christian axioms. You'll find it can't be done!

The Manichaeans

While the Roman Empire was collapsing under its planned economy, the Christian Church emerged from the chaos as the only coherent group. Under its protection, individual freedom and initiative were encouraged within limits, especially in the noncontroversial areas of art and scientific abstraction.

But the viewpoint persisted that God's kingdom should assume the form of an earthly monarchy, and there were various conflicts and compromises between the Church and the living authorities.

Persons act in accordance with their beliefs. So far as the laws of physics permit, they create a human world in the image of their God or gods. Medieval Europeans held the pagan belief that an authority controls all men in a static universe.

During the early Christian centuries, most Europeans were followers of Manes — a reformer of the ancient sun worship whose teachings had swept Europe in a wave of religious enthusiasm. They were known as Manichaeans, and they looked upon the universe, not as a unit, but as a vast battleground of conflicting forces. They saw everything in terms of opposites. There was war between light and dark, between good and evil, between soul and body, heat and cold, wet and dry, up and down. War was the natural order of things. It was everywhere and among all things, including men.

Although, as time went on, most of the Manichaeans turned to Christianity, they did not give up their pagan views. They continued to believe that an authority controlled them. They continued to think in terms of opposites. They had no difficulty in accepting the two conflicting views that man is free and that man is not free; that on the one hand, the individual person is self-controlling and on the other hand, he is controlled by great powers outside himself.

Thus, when the Manichaean became a Christian, he believed that his soul belonged to God — or, if he were not careful, to Satan — and that his body belonged to his master. Just where he himself came into the picture isn't quite clear. But the fact remains that during ages of misery and human degradation, the Church kept alive the principles of common decency, morality, and humaneness — the recognition of human rights and the brotherhood of man.

The Feudal System

The advance of Christianity in Europe resulted in the rise of the feudal system. Under this system, people lived in an invisible world where space and time were not real but where all souls were equal.

Outside the Church, the system was one which men could not endure unless they wholly believed that the universe is static. They could never have borne its stagnating effects if they had ever imagined progress. But they truly thought of the material world as a temporary waiting room — which needn't be comfortable because one passes through it only on a journey — and that any hardships or inequalities would bring future compensations.

In a sense, the feudal system resembled communism, except that it was set up on a stratified basis. In theory, each class contributed according to its abilities and received according to its needs, which were gauged by the social position of the particular group. Obviously, since the knight's lady needed a horse to ride, it was only fair and proper that the serf should yoke his wife to the plow.

The absence of responsibility and the freedom from the urge of ambition were not without their compensations. Discontent was reduced, and each class had some degree of economic security. Fastened to the land, a serf could neither leave it nor lose it. He worked it as he was told. He had a fixed share of any crop God might will. He could not risk or lose or gain anything. If another baron seized the land, the serf, as a part of the booty, stayed right on.

Every man had a fixed place in the structure. As a part

of his class, he owed a certain duty to each other class and received from each a certain return. Barons owed training and leadership to their knights. Knights owed military service to their barons. Serfs and peasants worked the land and produced all the necessities of life for the upper classes, from whom they, in turn, received protection and justice.

War was the rule rather than the exception, and it raged across the feudal countryside throughout the Dark Ages. But the fighting of wars was on a highly professional basis. It was the sole and exclusive business of knights and barons, and they attended strictly to it — taking only a little time out on Saturday afternoons for a few innocent rounds of highway robbery.

Hunger and famine were also normal. Frequently God's wrath, they thought, descended in frightful epidemics of cholera, typhus, bubonic plague; and while lords and ladies fled to house parties on the beautiful countryside, the lower classes died so swiftly that the survivors couldn't bury the corpses.

Progress

But the specialization of effort and the systematizing of war made it possible for human energy to work with some degree of effectiveness. Famines became less frequent. Some of the peasants grew so prosperous that they even wore shoes on holidays, when merry crowds thronged to watch men and women burned alive at the stake, broken on the wheel, or hanged, drawn, and quartered. Craftsmen and artists built beautiful Gothic cathedrals, and nobody minded living huddled around them with few comforts and less sanitation than cattle in pens.

But in spite of its drawbacks, the feudal system was one of the most highly perfected forms of social-economic organization in history. It even had a sort of safety valve to release any undue pressure of energy. A highly gifted boy, even of the lowest class, might, with his master's permission, learn to read and write so that he could enter the Church. The discipline was strict in the Church, but all men were equal there. Any priest might become a pope; the son of a peasant actually did become a pope.

From the Dark Ages

It was under the feudal system that Europe emerged from the Dark Ages. It is held by some that the height of Old World civilization was reached under the feudal system. But in Continental Europe, only three or four short-lived generations enjoyed the benefits of this perfection. After that, there followed a period of confusion which the textbooks describe as the "rise of nationalism."

Some of the barons managed to steal a march on other barons and to make themselves kings, and the other barons didn't quite relish the idea of taking orders from a former fellow-baron. The skirmishes on the countryside were supplanted by major wars between ambitious nations, and the peasants were called from their plows to follow the banners of nationalism.

Even in Catholic countries, Europeans began to accept the theory that the king partakes of the divinity of God and that the child of a king is the natural heir to this divine endowment. This compromise was a backward step. In Europe, it wrecked the feudal system, the existence of which depended on maintaining a communal balance between classes. The reversion to pagan beliefs upset this balance and resulted in nationalism and war.

Magna Charta

Only in Britain was the feudal system kept intact — properly balanced and improved. On their sea-guarded island, the British barons successfully resisted their kings. At Runnymede in the year 1215, their armed forces so frightened King John that he signed an agreement to respect feudal customs.

The Magna Charta was an admission from the King that his power was not unlimited. As a written statement of British liberties, it has preserved the best values of the feudal system and has served as the foundation for building the British Empire.

But a grant of freedom is a denial of the fact that the individual is naturally free. A thing that can be given to one person by another person can also be taken away.*

The point is that freedom exists in nature; it is the individual person's inherent, inalienable self-control — a natural function of the human being. It is the same as life itself. Man is endowed with liberty by the Creator, just as he is endowed with life and with the power of reason.

To speak of liberty as a *grant of permission* — by one person to another person or by a so-called government to

*In France, Hungary, and Spain, the kings also signed "Magna Chartas," but these were repudiated by later kings.

its so-called subjects — is within itself a denial of the principle of individual freedom. Such a denial is based on the assumption that human beings are incapable of taking care of themselves; that they must be held sub-servient to an authority which controls their actions and is responsible for their welfare.

Industry and Commerce

The English modified this pagan belief as far as it could be modified under the feudal system; and while other governments used military force to enlarge the area of their rule, the British merely permitted its traders to trade.

In a world of war-made empires, the British — with the exception of their few lapses into arbitrary planning and their stupid interference with the early American col-onies — have used force primarily to protect the essential functions of industry and commerce.

Continental Europeans, whose ancestors abandoned the human values of feudalism, are inclined to sneer at the English as a nation of shopkeepers and hypocrites. But only the English — by granting to each individual the human rights within his class — have stood for the true values of feudalism.

British authority, in contrast to that of ancient Rome, is tempered with a quality of humaneness. British laws, based on the Ten Commandments, are designed to pro-tect the individual and are administered with a fine sense of equity and with a consideration of human rights.

The solitary colonial administrator — full of fever and quinine, in topee and mosquito boots — doggedly does his duty, looking after the savages under his care. He claims no more for himself than his own human rights *in his own class*. He does not regard the savage as his social equal, any more than he considers himself to be the social equal of an earl. In the sight of God and British justice, all men are equal — and in this world, each man has his place.

Although founded on inconsistencies, British feudalism, tempered with the British sense of fair play, made a greater contribution to progress than can ever be expected from any trend toward Marxism.

But so much for the compromises which are presented as a background for the second and third attempts to establish individual freedom. While Europe was still stagnating in the Dark Ages — and several centuries before Britain had its Magna Charta — a dynamic but little-known civilization, based on a recognition of personal freedom, was blazing in the Near East and spreading along the shores of the Mediterranean.

Chapter 10

THE SECOND ATTEMPT

ABOUT 1,400 years ago, a self-made businessman began the second major attempt to establish individual freedom. Born in the year 570 A.D., he was an orphan — of good family, but cheated out of his property inheritance. As a child, barefoot, ragged, and hungry, he worked 16 to 18 hours a day and slept on the bare ground under the sky. He had no schooling, but he had practical ability. He got ahead and, as time went on, became widely known and respected. He traveled, buying and selling goods throughout the greater part of the then-civilized world.

Babylon was long forgotten, and the Roman Empire had ceased to exist. Europe, sunk in the barbarism of the Dark Ages, was less important than Africa is today. Constantinople — surrounded by the thriving cities of Baghdad, Damascus, Antioch, Alexandria — had become the center of world trade.

To understand this man, think of a seasoned business executive of today who earns, say, $25,000 a year — a sufficient but not spectacular success. Shrewd, humorous, and friendly, he is more interested in human relations than in problems of trade. He marries his employer, a woman of business ability. Comfortably well-off at middle age, they retire to live, let's say, in Miami.

He and his wife keep open house. They serve coffee to

their friends. The entertainment is conversation. The host's opinions are so unusual that for some three years he is rather reserved in stating his views, lest they sound too radical. But little by little, he begins to express himself more openly, and friendly arguments originating in his living room begin to spread over the town.

He agrees with Abraham and Christ: The pagan gods do not exist; there is only one God — the God of Truth and Rightness — who judges men but does not control them; each individual is self-controlling and responsible for his own acts; all men are brothers.

Radical Blasphemy

The man's name was Mohammed. His ideas created terrific excitement because he was expressing them in Mecca, the shrine of the most renowned pagan gods.

From far and wide, pilgrims came to Mecca to worship a strange, heavy, black stone which was believed to have descended from the heavens. Lesser gods surrounded it, and the most famous poets of the day displayed their rhymes in the holy *Kaaba* that sheltered the sacred stone. Mecca made its living by serving pilgrims, just as Miami is supported by tourists. So Mohammed's blasphemy not only shocked the more devout Meccans, but also the merchants and tradesmen had grave misgivings as to its effect on business.

But Mohammed went right on saying what he thought, pointing out that Abraham, Moses, and Christ had stated these same truths. He was convinced that the priests had corrupted Abraham's teachings when they assumed authority over the Jews. Christ had attacked the priests and reasserted the truth. Now the priests were corrupting the teachings of Christ by assuming a controlling authority over the Christians. Mohammed concluded that formal organization brings the danger of corruption; that each person is responsible directly to himself for his thoughts, speech, and acts; that God will do the judging.

Sanctuary

The pagan priests pronounced their most blasting curses against Mohammed, but to no avail. The plain people thronged to Mohammed's home in increasing numbers. The more "respectable" Meccans were increasingly alarmed, but Mecca was a sanctuary in which no blood might be shed. The subversive elements were not to be killed. All that might be done was to harass them, in the hope that they would leave. Many of Mohammed's followers did leave, but this had an effect opposite to what had been hoped. Those who left spread Mohammed's ideas to other places; and many visitors to Mecca spent their time listening to Mohammed instead of worshiping at the shrine of *Kaaba*.

Then, in spite of the ban against bloodshed in the holy sanctuary, Mecca's more respectable citizens — including the tradesmen — took the law into their own hands. They organized a vigilance committee and stormed Mohammed's home with drawn knives and sabers.

But Mohammed was no longer there. Together with his family and companions, without haste or confusion, he had made tracks for the South. Hot on the trail, the Meccans pursued him; but Mohammed, this time without leaving any tracks, had swung leisurely northward.

He was headed for Medina, a small town in the palm groves, where people lived mostly on the date harvest and flocks of goats and sheep. For some time past, he had had a standing offer to come there and be its emir.

Medina was situated on an important road to Mecca. An increasing number of pilgrims stopped off to hear Mohammed, and he converted them to the belief that there is but one God and that the Meccans were idolators. This had serious economic repercussions. Mecca's income was cut at its roots, and the city crashed into its worst depression. Its people concluded that they could not live in the same world with Mohammed's ideology. Failing to realize that killing Mohammed would not kill his ideas, they prepared for war and set out to destroy Medina.

A Military Miracle

With archers, spearmen, and cavalry far outnumbering the total population of Medina, they quietly approached its outskirts before dawn. There was no sign of resistance. The little town lay quiet and sleeping, unaware of the impending danger.

The Meccan cavalry deployed, and, suddenly howling their war cry, they charged head-on. Then out of nowhere their onslaught was met with a terrific barrage of arrows, bringing down horses and riders in mid-charge. The attacking cavalry dissolved in a welter of fallen, dying, and dead. The survivors pulled out of it in confusion and took another look. But Medina still lay quietly sleeping, with not a defender in sight. This was a miracle! Nothing like it had ever happened before.

Mohammed had invented a new type of warfare. His

men were hidden in trenches which completely surrounded the town. To charge into a trench was suicide. To leap it was to be surrounded. Volleys of arrows were futile—most of them sped only to earth.

The Meccans withdrew and tried to figure things out. Then, after a long period of consultation, they galloped furiously back and forth before the trenches—but beyond arrow-range—yelling threats and insults and daring the Medinans to come out and fight like men. Nobody did.

This went on for days. The Medinans had ample provisions and water. The Meccans soon consumed theirs. Finally, at their wits' end and unable to think of anything else to do, they turned back toward Mecca, 200 miles away.

News of their unfought war probably reached there ahead of them. Certainly it traveled with the caravans as fast as camels could go—it was the kind of news that no one forgets to tell. Soon it had spread to all the bazaars of India, China, Persia, Arabia, Byzantium, Palestine, all northern Africa, and to every oasis in the Sahara.

After six years in Medina, Mohammed traveled back to Mecca as a peaceful pilgrim—but prudently accompanied by 30,000 good fighting men, amply armed. A deputation met him outside the city to welcome him to the holy sanctuary, in which no blood might be shed. The Meccans accepted his religion, and the pagan idols were removed from the *Kaaba* (630 A.D.). Two years later, Mohammed died.

Historians have never seemed able to explain the terrific expansive force of Mohammed's influence. Carlyle marvels: ". . . as if a spark had fallen, one spark, on a world of what seemed black unnoticeable sand; but lo, the sand proves explosive powder, blazes heaven-high from Delhi to Grenada!"[6]

Contributions of the Saracens

Schoolbooks lay great emphasis on European history, ancient and modern; but no point is made of the fact that, when Europe was stagnating in the so-called Dark Ages, the world was actually bright with a civilization more closely akin to what we have in America than anything that had gone before. Thirty generations of human beings who believed in personal freedom created that civilization and kept it going for 800 years.

In the deserts and the mountains and the steamy fertile river valleys, from the Ganges to the Atlantic, these people were of all races and colors and classes, all creeds, all former cultures, all former empires. They included Buddhists, Christians, Moslems, Jews, Hindus, Mongolians, Chaldeans, Assyrians, Armenians, Persians, Medes, Arabs, Greeks, Egyptians, Phoenicians, Hittites, Africans, and hundreds of others whose ancient ancestors had worn the soil to dust before the earliest dawn of history.

There is no one name that correctly applies to all of these people. The Europeans, who hated them, called them "Saracens."

The records of the much-maligned Saracens — their 800 years of civilization, their institutions, their methods, their ways of living — are locked in their common language, Arabic. Since American historians are European-minded, we get only glimpses of the Saracens' world, seen through European misunderstanding and bitterness dating back to the Crusades. Because of the deep-seated prejudice, and in the interest of fair play, it seems appropriate to swing the pendulum the other way and present the Saracens' side of the story.*

It is to the Saracens that the world of today owes much of its science — mathematics, astronomy, navigation, modern medicine and surgery, scientific agriculture — and their influence led to the discovery and exploration of America.

In the world of the Saracens, no authority suppressed scientists, and no policeman harried them — nor did any government take care of them. They opened schools; and from Baghdad to Granada, students flocked to them. Some of these schools grew into great universities, and for hundreds of years they continued to grow.

Learning versus Teaching

The Saracen universities had no formal organization — Mohammed contended that too much organization leads to corruption. The rules were few. There were no standardized programs, no regular curriculums, no examinations. To guard against the fallacious idea that education ends with graduation, the Saracens' schools granted no diplomas, no degrees. They were institutions, not of teaching, but of learning. Students went there to acquire knowledge, just as Americans go to grocery stores to buy food.

*This chapter is based mainly on information gathered by Rose Wilder Lane, whose researches include personal contacts among remnants of former Saracenic tribes. Almost everything in it should be in quotes, except that I have taken liberties in condensing Mrs. Lane's original text.

Classes were held on an open-house basis. Anyone in quest of knowledge was free to wander about and listen. If he decided to remain, he picked a teacher and privately discussed with him what he wanted to learn and what he should study, and they agreed upon a fee. If, after joining the class, he didn't get the knowledge he wanted, he stopped paying the teacher and went to another teacher or another university. When he had learned what he thought he ought to know, he quit school and put his new knowledge to practical test.

For 800 years, the Saracens' schools and universities proceeded on the principle of freedom — on the basis of voluntary agreement between teacher and student. They offered all the learning of the past, with special emphasis on scientific knowledge.

One of the outstanding characteristics of the Saracens was their ability to build on the experiences of others. They studied the works of Aristotle, Galen, Euclid. They took unto themselves the past discoveries and techniques of the Greeks, the Chinese, the Romans — and usually found ways to improve upon them.

For example, consider the question of numerals: The figures that you find on an adding machine, or on the upper row of typewriter keys, or on the pages of this book are known as Arabic numerals.

Although handed down to us by the Saracenic Arabs, our numerals are really of Hindu origin. The Greeks and the Romans had seen the Hindu symbols in India; but they stuck to the clumsy Roman numerals and continued to do their adding, subtracting, and multiplying by clicking little balls along wires, as the Chinese still do. Not so with the Saracens. They seized upon the simple Hindu numbers and improved them. It is only when people are free that they begin to look for labor-saving methods. (See page 218.)

Priceless Zero

Not the least of the Saracens' contributions to our modern civilization is that their free minds were first to grasp the mathematical concept that the absence of a number — nothing — is itself a number. They invented *zero*, without which science as we know it today could hardly exist.

Offhand, that may sound a bit far-fetched; but think it over, and ask yourself what would happen in this modern world of meticulous calculations if we were compelled to discard the ciphers and the decimal points and go back to Roman numerals.*

Having established the concept of zero, the Saracens proceeded to develop arithmetic. Then they added algebra, including quadratics. To Euclid's geometry, they added plane and spherical geometry and trigonometry. Applying these to sun, moon, and stars, they produced astronomy. They built observatories across three continents, studied the heavens, recorded their observations, and put them to practical use.

They deduced the shape of the earth and its move-

*Today, any mathematician will tell you that without zero, there could be no mathematics. Without zero, Americans could have no engineering, no chemistry, no astronomy, no adequate measurement of substance, time, or space. Without zero, there would be no skyscrapers, no subways, no modern bridges, no automobiles, no radios. There would be no rayon, no cellophane, no aluminum, no electric refrigeration, no atomic power. Without zero, there could be no modern science—no modern world.

ment around its axis and around the sun, and they gave to Europeans the information that the earth is round, along with calculations of its measurements. They invented the sextant and the magnetic compass, which made possible the navigation of their vessels on the open seas, beyond the sight of land.

They provided Christopher Columbus with the instruments and the charts which he took with him when he sailed west in search of a new route to India. The Saracens' calculations of latitude were very accurate, but of longitude not quite so good — which caused Columbus and his backers considerable embarrassment. (See page 138.)

The Saracen navigator of a thousand years ago would have little trouble understanding the charts and instruments on today's most modern ocean liner. He would see improvements, but the only instrument that might really baffle him is the gyrocompass. He would be able to use it all right, but he wouldn't understand the electric energy that keeps it spinning.

Advances in Medicine

Rivaling their work in astronomy and navigation, the Saracens made important contributions in the field of health and sanitation. They translated Galen's works into Arabic for use in their schools and did original research in medicine and surgery. Nine hundred years ago, they were using the medical pharmacopoeia of today, excepting only the recently discovered chemical compounds. There was not another great advance in medicine from the time of the Saracens until the American century.

[108]

From the Ganges to the Atlantic, they built medical schools and hospitals. While one of these was flourishing at Salerno, Italians a little farther north are credited with doing the first surgical operations ever performed in Europe. Since dissection was forbidden in Europe, the Italians doubtlessly learned their anatomy from the Saracens. Surely no doctor, even in the Dark Ages, would have had the nerve to cut open a patient without some notion of what he was going to find inside.

It was the Saracens who discovered the local anesthetics used in these operations. The next great attack upon pain was the discovery of general anesthesia, first used in a surgical operation by Dr. Crawford Long in 1842, at Jefferson, Georgia.

In the 13th century, the doges of Venice are credited with the introduction of quarantine against contagious disease — and that also was out of keeping with the religious thought then prevailing in Europe, which held pestilence to be God's punishment for sin.

The explanation lies in the fact that the thriving city of Venice was carrying on a prosperous trade with the realistic Saracens. Indeed, it is significant that the whole Renaissance, the so-called "revival of learning" in Europe, should have arisen so inexplicably in the long, narrow peninsula of Italy, with Saracen civilization brilliant at its tip and with its every port opening into the Saracens' sea.

The Saracens Invade Europe

Precisely 100 years after Mohammed died, some of the Saracens moved into central France. A frantically assembled European army attacked and stopped them near Tours; but they remained in southern France and in Spain. The fanatic Europeans looked upon them as followers of the Antichrist—the mystic body of Satan on earth—and the Saracens regarded the Europeans as crude barbarians.

In Spain—at Cordova, Granada, and Seville—the Saracens built great centers of learning and art, science, production, and commerce. From India and Africa and Cathay, students came to the universities in Spain; and from Spain, students went to the universities in Cairo, Baghdad, and Delhi.

Farmers in fertile southern Spain poured into the cities an increasing abundance of food and raw materials; and out of the cities poured an increasing wealth of woolens, linens, cottons, silks, mosaics, enamels, porcelains, glass, and gloves. Ships thronged the harbors—unloading spices and ivory and camphor from India, tempered steel and wrought silver and brass from Damascus, horses from Arabia, and saddles of leather softer than velvet from Morocco.

Five Centuries of Progress

Progress continued for 500 years, until Saracenic Spain was three times as old as the United States is today. Then from darkest Europe, a half-million fighting men set out to attack the Saracens in faraway Palestine.

This unprovoked aggression began a world war which lasted until the United States Marines subdued the Barbary Pirates in the Mediterranean harbor of Tripoli in the year 1804. Pirates they were, but they didn't know it.

They thought they were still fighting the war which the Europeans had launched against their forefathers.

The Crusades

For more than a century, officials of the Church had been trying their best to make peace in Europe. First, they decreed the "Peace of God," but no one paid any attention. Then they declared the "Truce of God," which called for a long week end lasting from Wednesday night until Monday morning.

The idea was to induce the ruling classes — the barons and the knights — to take that much time out from their fighting, giving the farmers and craftsmen and traders a chance to work in peace and perhaps provide enough food to keep things going. But on Monday, Tuesday, and Wednesday, the barons and the knights could get on with the job of fighting for their frontiers, killing off useful peasants and serfs in the process.

It was a good idea, but it didn't work out because the Church was not strong enough to enforce it.

So Pope Urban II, perhaps in sheer desperation, summoned all the barons to a great council and made a speech that roused them to frenzy. He called on them to put aside their petty quarrels and to unite in a common cause — to free the Holy Land. He offered forgiveness of all sins to every man who enlisted, and he promised eternal reward to any who died in the effort. His speech deeply moved his listeners and aroused a natural yearning to get out of Europe and into heaven. The result was an outburst of fervor and fanaticism, the like of which the world has never known — before or since.

The Saracens had held the Holy Land for 500 years; and during all that time, Christians had worshiped unmolested at its Christian shrines. Jerusalem has always been a holy city to Moslems, who have a deep reverence for Abraham, Moses, Gideon, Samuel, and Christ. Christian shrines are also Moslem shrines.*

But these facts were evidently unknown to the Crusaders, who were dominated by the spirit of the vigilance committee run amuck.

After killing Jews and nonbelievers all through the Germanies, nearly half a million Crusaders crossed the Bosporus into Turkey. They besieged Nicaea, but the Christian Emperor in Constantinople allied himself with the Saracens and sent his troops to defend the city.

On to Antioch

Then the Crusaders moved on to ancient Antioch. They devastated the country so thoroughly that they themselves almost starved. It is reported that under the eyes of the guards on Antioch's walls, some of them cooked and ate the flesh of Saracens they had killed. They were unable to take the city by force, but a Christian com-

*According to Mrs. Lane, a Moslem has stood guard at the Church of the Holy Sepulchre night and day for a thousand years, except at Easter — and still did when she was in Jerusalem. On Easter Day, the guard retires so that no Moslem presence profanes this holy time. Christians of all rival sects crowd the dark cavern of the church, each group allotted its space. Then, in the black dark, the miracle occurs — fire bursts from the tomb. Rushing to catch the miraculous flame on their candles, the sects trespass on space allotted to others; and in murderous fury, Christians fight Christians, and blood flows in the Holy Sepulchre. Then at sunset, when Easter Day is over, the Moslem guard returns, and all is peaceful for another year.

mander of the Moslem troops let them in secretly by night. They massacred most of the population; and while bodies rotted in the streets and wells, a mysterious sickness came upon them.

As they resumed their march toward Jerusalem, they were astonished to find that the homes and villages along the way were deserted. How had the Saracens known they were coming? This was a land of devils and black magic. Their worst suspicions were confirmed when an envoy from the Sultan of faraway Egypt met them en route with a conciliatory message which urged that they fulfill their vow to the Pope and enter Jerusalem as peaceful and welcome pilgrims.

South of Beirut, they saw the black magic with their own eyes. In the sky, a hawk had wounded a pigeon. The pigeon fell to the ground. The incredulous Crusaders found, attached to its leg, a silver cylinder which contained a bit of paper bearing mysterious writing. A Syrian Christian guide translated it for them:

"The Amir of Akka to the lord of Caesaria, greeting. A race of dogs, stupid and quarrelsome, hath passed by me, marching without order. As thou lovest the Faith, do what thou mayest, and have others do, all that may hurt them. Send this word to other citadels and fortresses."[7]

The Massacre at Jerusalem

In two years, the Crusaders had fought only two battles and a few skirmishes. They had unsuccessfully besieged two cities and had taken Antioch by treachery. Out of almost 500,000 invaders, only 30,000 reached Palestine.

There they found palm groves, vineyards, and orchards of figs and sweet pomegranates; but the villages and towns and white-walled Ramleh were deserted. A hundred Crusaders rode into Bethlehem and found it to be a Christian town, built around the Cathedral of the Virgin Mary. Monks and priests entertained them royally. Then they rode back toward Jerusalem and came to the peaceful Church of the Blessed Mother of Christ, in the ancient Garden of Gethsemane on the Mount of Olives.

For five weeks, they attacked gray-walled Jerusalem. They hauled timbers from 30 miles away and built movable battle towers. Under a rain of boiling pitch and Greek fire, they advanced their towers and rushed across blazing drawbridges to engage in hand-to-hand fighting on the walls. They took the city; and for two days and nights, they slaughtered men, women, and children in houses and in churches, down alleys, over roofs. On the sunken pavement around the Mosque of Omar, their horses charged fetlock-deep in human blood.

Only one little group of citizens survived the massacre. They were of Christian faith. Huddled together, awaiting death, unable to speak the foreign tongue of the bloody killers, they sang a mass in Greek; the Crusaders, recognizing the tune, swerved by and left them alive.

Peaceful Christians

The Crusaders found Christians everywhere they went — for the simple reason that Christians had been there all along. For a thousand years, Christians had been living peacefully among the Moslems, along with Armenians, Albanians, Greeks, Copts, Marenites, Druses, Jews,

Parsis, Hindus, to mention a few. "Let there be no violence in religion," Mohammed had cautioned. ". . . fight for the religion of God against those who fight against you; but transgress not by attacking them first."[8]

It was the Europeans who had the habit of starting wars; it was the Europeans who massacred heretics, down to the last infant. They killed the Albigenses, the Waldenses, the Socinians, the Huguenots, the Covenanters, and many others. Five hundred years after the Crusades, both Protestants and Catholics were alternately seeking refuge in the American wilderness to save their lives from European fanaticism.

Before taking Jerusalem, the Crusaders met the Saracens only once in open battle. From then on, they respected them. In contrast to the bludgeoning Europeans, they wore light helmets of damascene steel, and their body-armor was of gilded steel mesh, which would turn the swiftest arrow but which was so sheer that a whole suit of it crumpled into scarcely more than a handful. The Saracen fighters were lean, agile, quick. Their horses were small and swift; their swords, thin and flexible.

The iron-armored ranks of Christendom would charge forward with the full-throated roar: "God wills it!" But the Saracens, flying their green silk banners, swept in like a wave and struck at the flank, with a ululating cry that sounded to the Crusaders like the howl of wolves: "*La ilaha illa-l Lah*" — There is but one God!

Bewildering Discoveries

When the Crusaders left Jerusalem to attack Ascalon, they were already adopting the Saracens' battle tactics.

But they were still unable to guess the uses of their loot. At Antioch, their bewilderment had been pitiable. They sat down on beds and leaped up terrified by the movement beneath them — they had never seen a mattress before. They were mystified by the draperies, carpets, cushions, leathers, linens; by magical chiffons that clung like cobwebs to their fingers and a silk that changed its color in the light.

The unknown metals and strange utensils were equally puzzling. Gingerly they sniffed at flaming liquids in queer containers — they had never seen an oil lamp before. They tasted and spat out a white powder, delicious but perhaps poisonous — it was sugar. In small gold boxes, they found tubes with jewelled stoppers, containing other strong-tasting substances. How could they understand cosmetics? The cosmetics used by the Saracen women were quite similar to those of today. No other women in history were so well-groomed, until the present generation of Americans.

Contrasts

In contrast to the European castles, with their rude stone walls and their floors littered with rotting reeds and bones, the Crusaders came into rooms that were like jewels — with tile floors and mosaic ceilings. Faintly scented air came through delicate latticework windows which permitted one to look out, though no one could look in. The lattice was of sandalwood.

Rummaging and wondering, dragging out and killing some quivering thing — a child or a slave — the invaders came upon cups which they mistook for rare jewels and which, in their excited grips, they crushed to splinters that cut the hand. For the first time, they learned about glass.

This, indeed, was a country of demons and devils; all Europe heard that it was.

Saracenic Cleanliness

The most amazing thing to the Crusaders, however, must have been the cleanliness. It seemed that everyone was always bathing. The Crusader knew what it was to get wet in the rain or when crossing a river, and the knight recalled the formal bath that had been a part of the ceremonial into knighthood. But the heathen Moslem bathed five times a day.

It was Mohammed's idea; he was almost fanatically clean. Probably in reaction from the filthy Christian ascetics of the time, he insisted that a clean, healthy body is essential to a clear mind and a pure spirit; and as a part of his plan to keep religion on an informal, personalized basis, he tied physical cleanliness to prayer. Let every man repeat five times daily the truth that there is but one God — no pagan gods — and before saying this, let him wash in running water. He pointed out that one cannot wash clean in standing water because it becomes dirty. Then, with a practical eye to trade, he added that men traveling through the deserts should scrub themselves with sand.

So the Crusaders came into a country where everyone was clean. Fountains were everywhere. Moslems sensibly did not interrupt business to recall that there are no pagan gods — they bathed and repeated that fact in their streets and bazaars. Anyone who wanted a fountain built one. Everything was on the basis of individual initiative and voluntary co-operation.*

Mosques were built in the same spontaneous way. There was no more organization about a mosque than there was about a Saracen university. Men in the neighborhood kept the mosque in repair if they liked; if they didn't, it fell into ruin in time. Philosophers, poets, and idlers sat in its quiet courtyard, by its splashing fountain. At dawn, noon, and sunset, and in mid-morning and mid-afternoon, someone climbed the minaret and called out that there is no god but God. Beneath him in the city or countryside, everyone paused and repeated the fact. Some repeated it in the mosque, after bathing at its fountain; someone may or may not have read aloud from the Koran.

Prosperity in the Dark Ages

Theirs was a spontaneous religion based on a sense of reality, springing from and depending upon the personal self. And for 800 years, during the period when the greater part of Europe was submerged in the Dark Ages, this religion produced the most brilliant scientific prog-

*It should be borne in mind that Mohammed lived in the period 570-632 A.D. — about 800 years before the art of printing began to gain headway. Thus, his teachings have been variously interpreted and confused with the superstition and mysticism that characterized the Dark Ages. For example, the story of his going to the mountain when the mountain would not come to him probably had its origin in Mohammed's insistence that the individual should do things for himself, instead of waiting for help from the supernatural — or from men in public office.

ress and the greatest material prosperity that had ever been known to man.

Imagine the crusading knight who, after grabbing a kingdom in Syria, is dining for the first time in the palace of a neighboring emir. The knight is wearing harsh leather, coarse wool, and 80 pounds of iron armor on his unwashed body. He is in the habit of gnawing meat from a bone, tossing the bone over his shoulder to the dogs, then wiping greasy hands on his sleeves and guzzling down a hornful of ale. The courtyards, halls, and rooms no longer amaze him. They are like those he has looted. But what will he do when a servant offers him a silver bowl and holds poised above it a silver pitcher?

Before the Saracen ate, rose-scented water was poured over his hands, and he wiped them on linen damask or terry cloth — our bath towel. A servant placed an inlaid metal tray between host and guest and set on it a porcelain bowl of food. The Saracen ate with his fingers, as did the European, but he did not wipe them on his clothes. After each course, he washed his fingers and dried them on a fresh towel.

Not one dog sat scratching fleas and whining for bones. The floor of polished stone was bright and shining. On a raised dais, the host and guest sat on thick oriental rugs which were richly colored and spotlessly clean. (When a Saracen entered a house, he left his shoes outside.)

Scientific Farming

The foods were amazing and strange. There was a variety of meats, cooked with seasonings and sauces. There were salads and ices. There was an unknown drink in tiny cups— coffee, sugared and spiced. No European had ever before seen such a variety of cereals, vegetables, and fruits — rice, spinach, asparagus, lemons, melons, peaches — produced by the world's first scientific farmers.

In Europe, oxen and women pulled wooden plows which merely scratched the earth, and the crop was whatever God might will. Half of the farm land always lay fallow — giving birth to a crop tires the earth, and it must rest.

But in the world of the Saracens, not an acre of arable land ever rested. From Cathay to the Atlantic, across three continents, the Saracen farmers were deep plowing and contour plowing, fertilizing, irrigating, and rotating crops. They poured into the markets an abundance of nearly every food that we have today and took in return a wealth of goods such as the world had never known before. These goods included damask linens, mohair, muslin, Syrian silks, morocco leather, oriental rugs, mosaics, inlaid woods, glassware, porcelains, enamels, filigree and wrought work in metals. Damascene steel was not equalled until very recently in the United States.

From the Saracens

We Americans owe directly to the Saracens our Californian and southwestern architecture, our cotton industry, our asphalt paving, and a long list of such things as beds, tables, table and bed linens, divans, sofas, glass, china, rugs, strawberries, peaches, ice cream. We speak Arabic when we say *mattress, cotton, talcum, sugar, coffee, sherbet, naphtha, gypsum, benzine.* Our cars are run, our streets are paved, our houses are furnished, and our bodies are clothed with things that the Saracens began to create a thousand years ago.

An Opportunity to Praise

Jerusalem was the first of the kingdoms established by the Crusaders, and the Christian kings were able to hold it with fewer than a hundred soldiers. As time went on, the invaders were dressing and living like Moslems. They melted into the civilization of the Saracens, and their sons grew up so tolerant that they raised no objection to Moslems worshiping in Christian churches.

But the new kingdoms set up by the Crusaders lasted less than a century; then the Emir of Palestine proposed an alliance with England. He offered his sister in marriage to Richard the Lion-Hearted, who was crusading at the time. But Richard was planning to return to England; and, in spite of all his lion-heartedness, he lacked the courage to face his fanatical subjects with a Moslem queen.

Upon his refusal, the Moslems attacked and took Jerusalem, but they did not sack it. As soon as its defenders surrendered, the Emir released his prisoners unharmed and gave them 40 days to dispose of their property and go back home. During these 40 days, the people of Jerusalem bitterly complained that the departing Christians were stealing everything in sight, and they demanded that the robbery be stopped. The Emir replied that if he stopped the robbery, the Christians would say that he had broken his word; but that if he did nothing to stop it, the Christians would have an opportunity to praise the goodness of the Moslem religion.

He left to the people the responsibility of protecting their individual property, and the Europeans got away with quite a lot of loot. But they also took back something that was of far greater value. It was the new concept of sportsmanship and gentility which they had learned from the Saracens.

Chivalry

Prior to the Crusades, it had never occurred to the invaders that a strong man need not be brutal.

The Saracens were fierce in battle, but they were not cruel. They did not kill the wounded; they did not torture their prisoners. When they struck down an opponent, it was not uncommon to help him up. (Read Sir Walter Scott.) They did not persecute Christians. They were honorable; they told the truth; they kept their word.

The English knights were especially impressed; and, due in no small measure to the lessons learned from the Saracens, the British aristocracy developed into one of the finest ruling classes the world has ever known.*

In the meantime, subversive ideas were leaking into Europe from Saracenic Spain. Travelers from south of the Pyrenees brought these ideas into France and the

*One of the returning Crusaders — an Englishman named Wilder, whose life had been chivalrously saved by an Arab foe — decreed that the name of his rescuer should be carried down through each succeeding generation of the Wilder family. Thus it is that Rose Wilder Lane's father bore the name Almanzo — the original was probably El Manzoor. I got this story, not from Mrs. Lane, but from one of the delightful children's books written by her mother, Laura Ingalls Wilder; and I suspect that the daughter's deep interest in the Saracens stems from the family tradition.

Germanies; and European scholars were corresponding with Saracen scholars in the Spanish universities.

One of these dangerous ideas was that the earth is round — a planet among many planets spinning in space. This was contrary to the accepted teachings of the time, which were based on the pagan belief that an authority controls all things, including men. Such heresies had to be suppressed, and in most of Europe they *were* suppressed.

But the Italians were prospering from their trade with the Saracens, and they continued to deal with these men of greater knowledge and wider experience. The Saracens had better methods of navigating ships, quicker ways of computing costs and adding up bills. They transacted their business affairs over great distances and with incredible swiftness.

Pony Express

A European who traveled 18 miles in one day had something to write home about — had he known how to write. But a Saracen thought nothing of sending a parcel 200 miles and getting back a receipt on the following day. A thousand years ago, the Saracens' pony express habitually covered 200 miles a day — anywhere on land, from the Atlantic to the Indian Ocean. In a pinch, it could do 2,000 miles in eight days. Such speed over such a distance was not equalled until the year 1860, when the pony express ran from St. Joseph, Missouri to San Francisco.

The Saracens' postal service was even swifter. Today you can see a remnant of it in Ragusa on the Dalmatian coast. Ragusa was one of the "free cities" which traders had set up in Italy just before the Renaissance. It is important to notice that trade — the exchange of material goods — is always an exercise of individual freedom. Production and trade are possible only to the extent that restraints upon personal freedom are absent.

All Were Welcome

These free cities were the only spots in Europe where men could manage their own affairs, and it was in these spots that religious freedom began to take root. While most of Europe was being torn by fanaticism and religious jealousies, traders of all faiths were building their churches in Ragusa — a Roman Catholic church, a Greek Catholic church, a Moslem mosque and fountain.

Even today, under the arcade of the ancient market place, above the door that once led to the offices of the city, can be seen a painting of Mother Ragusa — the free city. The colors are still clear and fresh. Grouped around Mother Ragusa's knees, and equally enclosed by her arms, are children of all peoples — Norman, Mongolian, African, Slavic, Levantine. Below the portrait stands a marble bench on which three judges sat to hear and judge in public any complaints brought before them. They represented the free city. They were bound to judge all men with equal justice.

Ragusa prospered enormously. Its merchants rivaled and often outstripped the Venetians. When an earthquake totally demolished the city in the 16th century, it was rebuilt so rapidly that its prosperity was hardly interrupted. Ragusa was so rich and powerful that Spain

sought the little city as an ally and ships from Ragusa
sailed with the Spanish Armada against England.

Pigeon Mail

When rebuilding their city after the earthquake, the
merchants improved its postal service. They built dovecots all along the top of the city's double walls, and thousands of pigeons flutter around them even today. In common with other Saracen cities, Ragusa required every
foreigner to contribute two carrier pigeons from his home
town as an entrance fee at the city gates. These pigeons
were filed in the dovecots under the name of their home
town. When ships from Ragusa went to sea or when caravans set out on the long road to China, they took with
them as many pigeons as might be required to pay the
entrance fees to other cities and to carry back their reports. By carrier-pigeon mail, the salesman reported sales,
trade news, business prospects, and his next address.
Back at the "home office" in Ragusa, the replies, in sealed
cylinders, were turned over to the pigeon master, who
then selected the proper pigeon to send to the salesman's
next address.

This highly efficient postal service covered land and
sea from Spain to India. For speed and privacy in communication, it was not surpassed until Alexander Graham
Bell invented the telephone.

Roman post roads are justly famous and were excellent
for their purpose — which was military. They were useful to the Roman state and to privileged families and
classes. What is not so well known is that the Saracens
built a network of highways to serve the practical needs

of commerce and to connect their cities, which are still among the most beautiful in the world.

While their architects were creating dreams in marble, their scholars collected and exchanged rare manuscripts, and their traders extended their businesses throughout the civilized world. And all these complexes of free human energies, operating across three continents, were geared to the speed of the pigeon's flight.

The dynamic civilization of the Saracens had never been equalled and was not surpassed until 300 years after it ceased to exist.

Why did it cease to exist? The answer or answers to that question should be highly valuable in advancing the American effort to establish the principles of freedom and liberty. Although hundreds of books have been written on the Egyptians, the Greeks, and the Romans, so far as I can discover no historical analyst has ever developed a realistic account of the rise and fall of the Saracenic civilization.

Important Lessons

Barriers of language and deep-seated prejudices handed down from the time of the Crusades have obscured the important lessons that might be learned from this second attempt to set men free. The difficulty is increased by the fact that some of the reasons for its success are interwoven with the causes of its failure.

On the positive side, it seems that the anarchy of the Saracens, in contrast to that of the Israelites, was surrounded by certain restraints and was tempered with a belief in human brotherhood.

The majority of the people who were drawn together in the world of the Saracens had already been living in groups. They brought to their new civilization the traditional customs and habits of human association and human brotherhood, which they had inherited from the wide diversity of tribes and empires previously existing in the vast area between the Ganges and the Atlantic.

Group Anarchy

Thus, their anarchy might be described as the anarchy of groups, rather than the anarchy of persons. Individuals were not prevented from acting freely; but it seems that most of them chose to remain in tribal and family groups, voluntarily obeying many forms of authority which could not have been enforced. The different groups kept their old customs and traditions. They increased the natural authority of parents over children and the natural influence of wise and able men. Workers, traders, scholars, and others formed fraternal groups. The Saracens were great "joiners."*

*This same tendency is strikingly characteristic of Americans, who, as the intellectuals sneeringly observe, are the greatest "joiners" on earth. The American "Babbitt" spontaneously creates literally tens of thousands of free and voluntary associations of persons acting together for some mutual purpose: ladies' aids, country clubs, fraternal orders, building and loan associations, mutual banks, farmers' co-operatives, labor unions, chambers of commerce, parent-teacher associations — the list is endless. These free associations form the fabric of American social life; nearly every American belongs to several of them. American industry and commerce are organized on this same basis of free, mutual co-operation. General Electric, General Motors, U. S. Steel, Bell Telephone, Standard Oil, and the smallest store with one clerk — all were created and are maintained by the free will of persons working together for some common purpose, voluntarily accepting some authority which is not and cannot be enforced upon a single one of them.

They accepted Mohammed's liberal views as rules of personal conduct and as guides to human association along informal lines. There were the emirs, who led their troops of volunteer militia and served as the political leaders for their groups; there were the caliphs — the word means successor (to Mohammed); and there were the cadis, or wise men, upon whom their neighbors relied for judgment.

Moslem Justice

Mrs. Lane observes:

"A Westerner who has seen a quarrel flare dangerously in an Arab bazaar will never forget it. One voice, one word, pierces that din of bargaining; the sound shocks the turmoil to utter silence. Out of it comes a mob-roar. 'Brothers! you are brothers! Moslems, remember you are brothers!' With that roar goes a mob-rush. Get out of it, quick.

"It is over in a moment. Scores of hands tear the quarreling men apart, snatch the knives from their fists or sashes. An unperturbed din of bargaining rises again, while small crowds of men who can leave their own affairs surround the angry men and go with them to the nearest Cadi, who, if he wants to keep his reputation for wisdom, must then and there settle the quarrel in a way that satisfies everyone's sense of justice.

"You admire the method, because it works. But it is not law.

"Actually it is the way men always, everywhere, keep the peace, when no one of them has a recognized right to use force. Then each one feels his responsibility. This is the way Americans kept the peace on the frontier, and keep it now on fishing and hunting trips and in clubrooms."[8-b]

Behind the Law

An essential difference between American and Saracenic civilizations appears in the marriage customs. Among the Saracens, marriage was made by family agreement, with the consent of the bride and groom. It was not a religious sacrament; nor was it a civil contract, although such a marriage included property settlements from both families. If it later became necessary to enforce the terms, it was up to the aggrieved family to do the enforcing as best it could. There was no legal machinery — no impersonal third party to whom the family might appeal. The only protection of property seems to have been possession of the property, personal honesty, and public opinion.

This is not so unusual as it may seem. Law or no law, always and everywhere, the basic protection of life and property is the general recognition of human rights — life, liberty, and ownership.

On the American frontier before there were any laws, settlers didn't bother to lock their cabins; and the average citizen of today is not often within sight of a policeman. But in a complex civilization, human nature being what it is, the need sometimes arises for an impersonal third party, and then the policeman is a handy person to have around. His existence is a symbol of law and order — a reminder that the "bad man" will not be tolerated.

The Saracens had no police force. No state defended

their civilization by military power. They had no civil law which men could rally to defend. There was no organization, no political structure, to hold together the millions of persons who for 800 years had been creating a vast and complex empire extending over three continents.

But in spite of their many shortcomings, there is no denying that the Saracens made a good "second attempt"; and it should be remembered that their civilization had its beginning, and reached its peak, during the period when Continental Europe was submerged in the barbarism of the Dark Ages.

But the days of the Saracens were numbered. Medieval Europeans had broken through the Pyrenees; and the spirit of the Crusaders — a white heat of religious fanaticism — was directed against the Saracens of Spain. Bloody killings, torture, purges, and mass deportation went on for years. At the mercy of the Inquisitors in the West and disrupted at its core by the barbarous attacks of the Turks, the world of the Saracens sank into stagnation.

But in the wake of this disintegration, there followed a highly significant result.

EDITOR'S NOTE: An authoritative study for those who desire more information on the Saracen story is *A History of the Intellectual Development of Europe*, by Dr. John William Draper of New York University. (New York: Harper & Brothers, 1876, 2 vols.) While the history of the Saracens is scattered throughout the book, Chapter II of Volume II is especially pertinent to the theme of Mr. Weaver's summary.

Chapter 11

PRELUDE TO THIRD ATTEMPT

THROUGH Italy, the Saracens had given to Europeans "the awakening of science and learning" which lifted them out of the Dark Ages; through Spain, the last of their energy led to the development of a new world. The discovery, exploration, and early colonization of America are closely connected with the Spanish Inquisition. As an instrument of Church discipline, the Inquisition had its beginning early in the 13th century, but south of the Pyrenees it met with considerable opposition.

The people of Spain were different from the Europeans. For hundreds of years, they had been living in an atmosphere of freedom and religious tolerance. But European ideas of bigotry, class hatred, and authoritarian control were leaking in from the north. The new monarchs, Ferdinand and Isabella, were interested in strengthening their power; so in 1480, the Inquisition was taken over as an instrument of government, under their personal supervision, supported by police and military force.

Just three years later, Christopher Columbus, having been turned down by the King of Portugal, made his proposal to Spain. But Ferdinand and Isabella were so busy waging war against the Moslems and the Jews that they had no time to bother with outside ventures.

Things dragged along for almost a decade, until January, 1492, when the last of the Saracenic strongholds fell. It was the beautiful city of Granada — the great center of learning, science, art, architecture, and commerce which the Saracens had been creating for 800 years. Worn down by starvation after a nine months' siege, Granada finally surrendered; and behind the trenches, in an army camp just outside Granada, Columbus finally closed the deal which was to change the course of world events.

The Saracens had now been divested of their political status, and their properties were being confiscated. But their influence, by reason of centuries of trade and intermarriage, was deeply ingrained; and the conflict between authority and freedom did not end with the fall of Granada.

Relentless Inquisitors

In the years following the discovery of America, the activities of the Spanish Inquisitors became so widespread and so relentless that even the most devout and highly respected Christian citizen could not be sure of escaping persecution. Thus, many citizens who would normally have stayed at home chose to join the Conquistadors rather than to run the risk of falling into the hands of the Inquisitors.*

But that's getting ahead of the story.

*In Spain, you were in trouble if someone dropped a hint that you were a Moslem sympathizer or casually remarked that your neck looked unusually clean. The informer didn't have to appear against you in person, but he received a share of your property if you were convicted. For intimate side lights, read the historical novel, *Captain from Castille* by Samuel Shellabarger (Boston: Little, Brown & Co., 1945).

As Mrs. Lane reminds us, Columbus did not discover America — at least, not in the usual sense. Irishmen, Danes, Norwegians, Basques, and at least one Spaniard had seen this continent ahead of Columbus. She suggests that Breton fishermen refilled their water casks every season from the streams of New England; and she tells of an ancient map — drawn several centuries before Columbus was born, and still preserved in Venice, Italy — which clearly and correctly shows the coast line of Newfoundland.

America had been reached any number of times by the northern route. From Britain or Norway, the distance to Iceland is about 600 miles; and from there on, it's a matter of island hopping. On exceptionally clear days, the mountains of Greenland are visible from Iceland. The distance is only 150 miles; and once having reached Greenland, it's not much of a jump to Baffin Island, then down the coast to Labrador and the shores of New England.

So it was only natural for Iceland to be the original gateway to the New World, and among the most daring feats of exploration are the early voyages across 600 miles of the North Atlantic before the time of the magnetic compass.

No one knows who first discovered Iceland; but it seems that in the year 330 B. C., a navigator named Pytheas made a voyage from Marseilles, France, through the Straits of Gibraltar, and northward past the British Isles to what was called "Ultima Thule" — which means the supposed end of the world.

Pytheas probably reached Iceland, but it doesn't necessarily follow that he was the original discoverer. According to folklore, land was known to exist in that part of the world even before his time.

Pre-Columbus Voyages

In his book, *Great Adventures and Explorations,*[*] Vilhjalmur Stefansson gives many interesting sidelights on the pre-Columbus voyages: Ancient records in China indicate that a seafaring monk, Hoei Sin, crossed the Pacific along the shore lines of Kamchatka and the Aleutian Islands, reaching the coast of Canadian British Columbia in the year 499 A.D. In about 550 A.D., an Irish priest named Brendan made a voyage to Greenland. Iceland was colonized in 870 A.D., and Greenland in 986 A.D. Leif Ericson, Thorfinn Karlsefni, and others reached the shores of North America during the period 1000-1010 A.D.

And Stefansson relates just one more startling fact: An ancient stone slab, discovered in recent years near Kensington, Minnesota, bears an inscription to the effect that a party of Scandinavian explorers penetrated to the very center of the North American continent in the year 1362 — more than a century before Columbus reached the east coast islands in the Caribbean.*

*This stone slab, called the Kensington Rune Stone, was found entwined in the roots of an aged tree stump in the year 1898, but for a long time it was used as the threshold for a farmer's barn. Then it came to the attention of Hjalmar Holand of Ephraim, Wisconsin, who has deciphered the inscription as follows:

"[We are] 8 Goths (Swedes) and 22 Norwegians on [an] exploration-journey from Vinland through (or across) the West (i.e., round about the West) We had camp by [a lake with] 2 skerries one day's journey north from this stone We were [out]

Yes, America had been discovered any number of times prior to 1492; but that's no discredit to Columbus. So far as is known, he was first to make the voyage by the southern route across the full expanse of the Atlantic — about 3,500 miles of open sea, as against the 600-mile jump to Iceland.

A New Route to India

Columbus was doubtlessly familiar with some of the earlier explorations. In 1477, he had made a voyage to Iceland, and perhaps beyond. But Columbus was not interested in discovering a new continent; he was trying to find a new route to India.

The Crusades had shown that the riches of the world were in the East, and Marco Polo had brought back fabulous reports on India and China. However, the eastern route was long, and the militant Turks blocked the way. Portuguese seamen were trying to find a passage around southern Africa. Others had suggested that it should be possible to reach the Orient by sailing westward across the Atlantic.

and fished one day After [when] we came home [we] found 10 [of our] men red with blood and dead AV[e] M[aria] Save [us] from evil"

That is the inscription on the face of the stone. On one edge are the lines:

"[We] have 10 of (our party) by the sea to look after our ships (or ship) 14 days — journey from this island [in the] year [of our Lord] 1362"

Mr. Holand has written a most interesting book about the Kensington Rune Stone and various other evidences of ancient Scandinavian exploration in the Hudson Bay area: *Westward from Vinland* (New York: Duell, Sloan & Pearce, 1940), p. 101.

Among the Saracens, it was common knowledge that the earth is round. They had taken the theories of Aristotle and other Greek philosophers, reduced them to scientific observations, and applied their findings to the practical problems of navigation. The Saracens' knowledge of astronomy had been passed along to the European scholars and was generally accepted by them, although they had to be cautious in expressing their views.

The authority of the European rulers was based on the idea of a static universe. To accept the newfangled notion that the earth spins in space would be to admit the possibility of energy, change, and progress. Such heretical doctrines had to be suppressed.

That is why Roger Bacon, the 13th century "father of modern science," spent much of his life in jail. That is why the discreet friends of Copernicus published his discoveries as mere "mathematical abstractions." That is why the less discreet, the more outspoken, the downright rambunctious Galileo fell into the hands of the Inquisitors and escaped torture only by retracting his statements.

Admiral of the Ocean Sea*

Columbus didn't discover that the earth is round any more than he discovered America, but that again is not to his discredit. He was quite a person. A combination of circumstances gave him his big opportunity; his experience, knowledge, energy, and perseverance enabled him to make the most of it — at least up to a point.

*This is the official title granted to Columbus by Ferdinand and Isabella.

Columbus was a Genoese sailor, born and raised among the seafaring Saracens. He was a man of vision and courage who possessed the qualities of an able navigator, a great explorer, a capable executive, and a top-notch promoter.

To the money-mad Ferdinand, Columbus held out promises of gold and riches. To the devout Isabella, he emphasized the opportunities for uniting the ends of the earth beneath the sign of the Cross. Himself a devout Christian and student of the Scriptures, Columbus "loved to apply the Sacred Scriptures to his own life and adventures."[10]

Columbus had such great confidence in his project that he refused to budge on his terms: a super-admiral's commission with all expenses paid in advance, vice-regal authority over all new lands he reached to be forever hereditary in his family, and 10 per cent of all valuable metals *ever* found in those lands to belong to him and his heirs forever.

His proposition was finally accepted by the Spanish monarchs, but not until after Columbus had threatened to open negotiations with France. Of course, the terms of the agreement were never fulfilled. Columbus was so busy with his job that he was unable to hold his own against the political intrigue of the Spanish court.

While on his third voyage, he was the victim of a whispering campaign which charged him with mismanagement of the Hispaniola colony.

A successor, sent over to relieve him of his colonial duties, put Columbus in chains and loaded him on a ship bound for Spain. As soon as the ship pulled out, its captain ordered the shackles removed; but Columbus, with quiet dignity, would not consent. "He had been chained in the Sovereigns' name and he would wear them until the Sovereigns ordered them removed."[10-a] According to his son Ferdinand, Columbus kept the shackles on display in his home up to the time of his death and expressed the wish that they be buried with him, as a memorial of the reward he received for his services.

But that again is getting ahead of the story.

Mishap in Longitude

On August 3, 1492, just seven months after the fall of Granada, Columbus sailed confidently westward in search of the East. This voyage, across thousands of miles of unknown sea, would hardly have been possible except for the magnetic compass developed by the Saracens. The maps and navigation charts used by Columbus were also based on information supplied by the Saracens. In longitude, the data was inaccurate by some 8,000 miles; and when the "spice islands" didn't appear where they were charted, he had to quell a mutiny.*

When land was finally sighted, it was approximately where the charts showed India to be, so he had no doubt that he had found a western route to India.

---

*The Saracens had never needed any such measurements. They were not interested in sailing around the world to reach India; they were already there. But following the voyage of Columbus, the need for accurate measurements of longitude became increasingly apparent. The problem was not solved until the middle of the 18th century when John Harrison, a Yorkshire carpenter, was awarded a £20,000 prize by the British government for the development of an accurate chronometer. This device made practical the ingenious idea of measuring longitude on the basis of a zero position arbitrarily established at Greenwich, England.

The Follow-through

Thus it was that Columbus discovered America. But as Mrs. Lane points out:

> "Columbus might have come and gone and made no more difference than Eric the Red . . . if human energy had not leaped from Saracenic Spain, if thousands of men had not taken their lives in their own hands and risked them, on their own responsibility, in the unknown."[3-c]

The "follow-through" had always been lacking. But after the voyage of Columbus, Spanish energy leaped the Atlantic. Thousands of men and women sailed with Cortes, Pizarro, Ponce de Leon, Coronado, Balboa, Magellan — all those explorers and Conquistadors who put this hemisphere on the map and led the way around the earth. Thousands marched with their leaders from the Gulf of Mexico to the Ohio River and from the Rio Grande to the Missouri, nearly meeting in Kansas in the year 1545 — just half a century after the Genoese sailor crossed the ocean and sighted an island which he mistook for India.

Discovered by Youngsters

Youngsters like Hernando de Soto, who, in his teens, rode away from home on a lean horse with only a sword and a spear and his fearless self-reliance — America was really discovered by hundreds and thousands of such young men. And they came only from the former land of the Saracens.

Europeans to the north could no longer doubt that the

earth is round, and they knew that the fabulously rich and strange half of it still waited to be explored. But for almost a century — for three generations — they did not stir.

Amerigo Vespucci, who put one over on Columbus and gave America his name, was born and raised in Florence, Italy. He worked first for Spain and later for Portugal.

Another man came sailing under the English flag, followed a little later by his son sailing under the same flag. But they were not Englishmen; they were Venetians. They are known to history as John and Sebastian Cabot, but their real name was "Caboto." Like Christopher Columbus, they hailed from the heart of the Saracens' Mediterranean.

But nothing came of their efforts until the early 17th century; and while England sank back into lethargy, the energetic Spaniards were making regular voyages to and from the new continent.

For almost 800 years, the people of Spain had been living in close association with the Saracens, in a civilization that did not prevent freedom of action and individual initiative. The Saracens were now being liquidated; but Spain still had some free cities, and its citizens were not European — at least, not yet.

The change being wrought by the Inquisition was only a change in meaning, and it was slow in showing its effects. The spirit of individual freedom was too deeply rooted to die out overnight, and the momentum of the energy that had been generated by the Saracens was applied to the outfitting of ships and armies. The germs of that energy were being destroyed; but wealth was beginning to flow in from the New World, and the current prosperity obscured the deeper significance of what was happening beneath the surface.

No Time for Theory

A prosperous glove manufacturer in Seville, say, would have seen no difference — except that business was on the boom. If anyone had tried to point out the danger, he doubtlessly would have replied: "Oh, that's just theory. I'm a busy man, and this is no time to bother with theories. The glove market was never better. I'm on my way right now to land a big government contract."

But the Inquisitors were expanding their operations. Some 2,000,000 Moslems remained in Spain, and the King's troops were called upon to make them Christians — at the point of the sword. Tortured, slaughtered, burned alive in their blazing houses, or rounded up when they fled, the surviving Moslems were converted. But they continued to follow their heathen customs, reading their Arabic books, playing their athletic games, wearing their silk robes, and bathing — always bathing.

Church and state strictly prohibited these practices. Police burned libraries and searched converts' homes for Arabic books to burn. They stopped the athletic games They converted the baths (our Turkish baths) to other uses or razed them to the ground. Bathing in homes was strictly prohibited.

Despite all the efforts of the police, it seemed that the converts, now called "Moriscos," did not wholly accept authority. They were suspected of bathing secretly. There was doubt as to their inner convictions. To discover what they really thought, the Inquisition was necessary.

Prompted by the best intentions, the Spanish monarchs and their Grand Inquisitor considered themselves responsible for the salvation of each individual. Those whose minds were corrupted had to be destroyed, just as a good farmer must destroy a tubercular cow to protect the health of the herd.

This responsibility had to be accompanied by the authority to control the beliefs of the Moriscos — but first it was necessary to know just what they believed. Psychological tests and lie-detectors had not been invented; torture was the only means of finding out. And torture often revealed a taint, even in the minds of some Spaniards who didn't realize that they had Moslem leanings. Freedom of thought was found to be more prevalent than anyone had suspected.

Reforming the Moriscos seemed a hopeless task; and even after a hundred years of the Inquisition, more than a million of them were still in Spain. Some of the more liberal churchmen advised the King to deport them, but others contended that such a course would only spread the infection. These people argued that the King should not consider just the local problem; that it was his duty to act for the common good; that he had a responsibility for the welfare of the world at large. Therefore, the Moriscos should all be killed.

In answer to the objection that there might be one true Christian among the lot, it was pointed out that any such victim would go immediately to heaven; so instead of inflicting an injustice, they would really be doing him a favor.

But the final decision was for mass deportation. The remaining Moriscos were driven from their homes and herded toward the ports. Beaten, robbed, murdered, or dying of hunger and thirst along the way, few of them lived to reach Africa, and so far as is known, none was left alive in Spain.

The Spanish intellectuals burst into a great song of hope and joy triumphant. Spain had been cleansed. It had accepted the European ideology. Its people were now united in one common belief — the belief that an authority controlled their lives and would henceforth be responsible for their welfare.

World Empire

The loss of a million persons was not decisive. Millions had died in Spain during its centuries of vigorous achievement, but millions were still alive in Spain.

On the surface, things were better in every way. Spain was no longer dependent on domestic industry. During the century following the fall of Granada, Spain had become the center of a great empire. The Conquistadors had crossed unknown oceans and seized 60 degrees of latitude and one-sixth of the earth's circumference. They had explored and conquered Cuba, the Caribbean Islands, Peru, Chile, New Granada, Venezuela, Central America, Mexico — sweeping northward to the Missouri River and westward to the Golden Gate.

In the Pacific, Spaniards had taken possession of the Philippines. In Europe, they held Portugal and the Low Countries and almost all of France. The King of France was a prisoner in Madrid. Spain now held the Balearic Islands and most of northern Africa. By inheritance and conquest, they controlled Sicily, Sardinia, Naples, Milan, and the Germanies. In the center of Europe, the Spanish monarch was Emperor of all these lands and people. In the West, he dominated England, which was under the rule of his daughter-in-law. In the East, his troops had met the Turks at Vienna and flung them back into the Balkans, defeated.

In a final burst of glory, Spain had built the first great world empire — an empire that all but encircled the globe.

History Repeats

But there was a weakness at the core. Not only had the energetic Moriscos been exterminated, but also for three generations the most self-reliant of Spain's young men had been leaving their native land to seek fame and fortune in the New World. Others had gone to the European wars.

The people at home had been won over to the alluring theory of authoritarian control. They were losing their self-reliance with their independence. As in the case of Greece and Rome, it was the beginning of the end. In three generations — from grandfather to grandson — the concept of individual freedom was all but forgotten.*

In the meantime, while Spain was busy strengthening its central government and extending its planned economy, England was drifting in the opposite direction.

---

* In social and economic phenomena affecting either the growth or the disintegration of a state, there is usually a long-drawn-out time interval between cause and effect. This has its parallel in the "shirt sleeves to shirt sleeves" adage. But when the facts are available, the starting point can be traced back to the time when things were done that tended to improve or impair the effective use of human energy.

Under the reign of Queen Elizabeth, the British government became so badly disorganized and so weak that the people were thrown on their own resources. It was "root hog or die," and private citizens rose to the occasion — with telling effects.

Unwittingly, without conscious intent and with no centralized planning, the foundation was being laid for a new empire based on trade and commerce. In the eyes of the European powers, England had degenerated into near-anarchy. But when the "invincible" Spanish Armada sailed forth to capture the island, Francis Drake and his hastily assembled fleet of motley privateers defeated them soundly.

It was a turning point in world history, and Spain never quite recovered.

Aftermath

The days of the Conquistadors were over. The Spanish colonies were beginning to stagnate under bureaucratic controls administered from faraway Madrid. The stream of riches which had been pouring in from the New World was slowing down. Domestic industry had almost ceased to exist. Government overhead was completely out-of-bounds.

Things went from bad to worse, and after two more generations the people of Spain were not getting enough food to keep alive. Unpaid soldiers left the frontiers unguarded and ravaged the countryside. Vast areas of fertile land were abandoned; the rural population flocked to the cities in search of food, just as a fisherman might seek dry land in a frantic effort to change his luck.

When people get into the habit of depending on some centralized authority to provide the things which they alone can produce, mob psychology always takes hold, and they flock to the cities.

The government could no longer get even a dribble of taxes from provinces which had formerly filled the royal treasury to overflowing. Tax collectors tore down private homes and sold the materials to raise money. In some towns, they demolished more than half the dwellings.

The King, in sheer desperation, slashed official salaries — even those of the highest nobles and members of the royal household. Then he slashed them again, but even at the greatly reduced rates, he couldn't meet his payroll.

The day of reckoning was at hand. For too long, the people had been lulled into false complacency. For too long, they had been taught to expect some centralized authority to run their lives and provide for their needs. Human energy had ceased to function. Spain, as a great power, had ceased to exist.

But across the sea, a new civilization was in the making — a civilization more closely resembling that of the Saracens than anything which had gone before.

Chapter 12

THE THIRD ATTEMPT

ABRAHAM and the prophets knew that men are free.
Christ knew it. The Saracens knew it. And 200 years after
the fall of Granada, the idea was gaining momentum
along the eastern edge of North America.

Obscure individuals — who lived and died unknown to
anyone but their neighbors — started the third attempt to
establish conditions in which human beings could use
their natural freedom.

This third revolutionary effort has hardly begun. There
are men living today whose grandfathers helped to begin
it. Yet it was started when gods in human form were believed to govern most of the earth's population; when
kings by divine right owned Continental Europe and
most of the New World.

Fewer than 3,000,000 persons lived in scattered settlements along the Atlantic coast, from Labrador to New
Spain (the Floridas). They were of all races, colors, an-
cestries, and creeds. The French were in the north and
in the Carolinas. The Dutch had built a village on Manhattan Island, and their frontier cabins extended into the
Mohawk Indian country, in what is now known as upper
New York State. Germans had settled in the Jerseys and
far to the west — even beyond Philadelphia. There were
Swedes in Delaware. Germans and Scotch-Irish were
climbing the mountains of Carolina. Massachusetts, the

New Hampshire grants, Connecticut, and Virginia had been settled by English, French, Dutch, and Irish.

Mingled with all these were Italians, Portuguese, Finns, Arabs, Armenians, Russians, Greeks, and Negroes from dozens of different African tribes and cultures; black, brown, yellow, and white; Roman Catholics, Greek Catholics, Protestants, Jews; aristocrats, freemen, bond servants, slaves — and in all groups and classes, there was intermarriage with the American Indians.

In the interest of historical perspective, it is important to remember that during more than half of our history, America was a conglomeration of colonial settlements — subservient to European powers and without any government of its own.

The Spanish

The Old World monarchs, eager to extend their domains into the New World, granted large tracts of land to favored subjects.

Spain had the edge by almost a hundred years and began setting up colonies on the American mainland as early as 1509. In the beginning, the efforts were rather loosely organized. The Conquistadors were going ahead on their own initiative — handling any problems that arose and settling them right on the spot. Things were moving too fast for the Madrid bureaucrats to keep up with the details.

But as time went on, the home office supervision was tightened up. Bureaucratic controls were extended to the farthest outposts and were strictly administered "for the common good."

Under the sponsorship of the government — and at the government's expense — carefully selected peasants of good character, sound morals, and industrious habits were shipped over and established on collectivist farms. The government provided detailed instructions for clearing the land, caring for fences and gates, plowing, planting, cultivating, harvesting, and dividing the crops.

By order of the King, each settler's family was given a six-month-old pig, a barrel of grain for each adult, and a hoe for every child over six years of age.

Each settlement was built as in Spain — a compact mass of cottages, protected by a detachment of soldiers and a well-constructed fort:* A commandant, appointed by the King, kept order and dispensed justice — usually with much sympathy and wisdom. Typically, he addressed the settlers as "my children," and they were obedient, well-behaved, and gay. They made friends with the Indians and learned their ball games, raced horses, fought cocks, danced, and sang. They were cared for as well as, or better than, their friends and relatives back home. Shipping was well organized; communication was fairly frequent. The Spanish colonists enjoyed a reasonable degree of safety and leisure in the American wilderness, and they usually had enough to eat.

---

*Through an unfortunate error made in Madrid, the Spanish government ordered the fort at St. Louis to be built on a site which the Missouri River flooded every spring. Even the children knew that the river's battering ice would destroy the fort, but orders were orders and must be obeyed. The fort was built. The morose Commandant drank himself into a stupor every day that winter. In the spring, the river demolished the fort, and St. Louis was unprotected when the British attacked it. Disaster seemed certain until a trader took command; under his voluntary leadership, the settlers put up a good fight and saved the town.

The French

Along the same pattern, the kings of France later established snug little settlements along the St. Lawrence
River; then around the Great Lakes and down the Mississippi Valley to New Orleans and Mobile; then up the
Ohio River to Fort Duquesne (Pittsburgh).

In common with the Spanish, the French settlers had
carefully planned programs, designed to extend their
homeland conditions into the New World.

Before Thomas Jefferson was born, there was a charming little Versailles in central Illinois. Aristocratic ladies
and gentlemen — perfumed and jeweled, bewigged, pow-
dered and patched — were carried by slaves in satin-lined
sedan chairs to Twelfth Night balls, while happy villagers, fatter than any in Europe, crowded outside the
windows to watch the gaiety.

The English

The English settlers were among the late arrivals; and
in contrast to the Spanish, French, and Dutch, they did
not have government sponsorship.

Britain was busy with domestic affairs and European
conflicts. Getting a foothold in the New World was
merely an incident; and in the beginning, things were
left very largely to the gentlemen adventurers and seafaring buccaneers who were willing to spend their own
money and take their own chances — with a nominal
share of the profits going to the Crown.

In the eyes of the carefully selected and well-regi-
mented French and Spanish, the English colonists were

a scandal. Their villages were unplanned. Their houses were scattered and far apart, instead of being built in orderly clusters according to the standard European pattern.

There was no co-ordination. They didn't cultivate their land communally. Their harvests were not shared equally. They had little respect for constituted authority.

The English colonies were often split up as a result of internal dissensions and clashing views. Rebels would pull out, push farther inland, and start new settlements. All in all, they were wild and undisciplined subjects of bad rulers; and to the Spanish and the French, the word *Bostonian* came to mean a lawless, devil-may-care sort of person — quite the opposite of what it means today.

But let's start at the beginning and quickly review how the English colonies got their start.

Sir Walter Raleigh

One of the earliest efforts was the result of a deal with the court favorite, Sir Walter Raleigh. In return for one-fifth of all the precious metals that might be found, Raleigh was granted the rights to the vast Atlantic seaboard region, which he named "Virginia" in honor of his Queen. It's interesting to note in passing that this financial arrangement was just the reverse of the policy followed by Ferdinand and Isabella. Columbus, who was financed by the Spanish government, was to get only 10 per cent — whereas Raleigh, who financed his own expeditions, was to get 80 per cent.

Raleigh made two unsuccessful attempts to establish a settlement on Roanoke Island, off the coast of North Carolina. After a brief stay, the first settlers insisted on being taken back to England. The next group was left stranded for almost three years; and when the supply ship finally arrived, the settlers had vanished. Just what happened to them is still a mystery, but many legends have evolved. Even today, among the Carolina foothills and westward as far as the Osage Mountains of Oklahoma, there are rugged individuals who swear that their ancestors were members of Raleigh's "lost colony" and that they simply moved to the mainland and up into the mountains.

After this disastrous experience, the English seem to have lost their enthusiasm. There were some reconnoitering voyages, but it was not until the early 17th century that any further colonization efforts were attempted.

Following in the footsteps of the religious — and profit-minded — Elizabeth, James I continued the practice of extending special privileges and land grants to private interests.

A few gentlemen, obtaining a colonization permit through political pull and agreeing to share their profits with the Crown, would organize a trading company at their own expense. Their agents would collect a shipload of ne'er-do-wells and make an agreement with them, which was usually broken by both sides.

The early English settlers were nothing to brag about. Successful men do not ordinarily bind themselves into servitude and leave home to vanish in a wilderness.

There were noteworthy exceptions which will be mentioned a little later; but for the moment, we are talking about the early beginnings in order to emphasize the difference between the English Colonies and the carefully planned settlements of other countries.

Rag, Tag, and Bobtail

It is no exaggeration to say that, in the main, the people sent over by the early trading companies were the rag, tag, and bobtail of Europe — hungry wretches lucky to be out of debtors' prisons, vagrants from highways and slums. They came at their own risk and with no guarantee of security.

Some of them were shanghaied; others sold themselves into slavery to pay for their passage. And there were shiploads of women who were auctioned off at the ports to settlers in need of wives.

The Spanish, French, and Dutch came over in order to extend the power of their home governments; but the English, more often than not, came over to escape the domination of the Old World monarchs. Among them were people in search of greater religious freedom, including the Pilgrims and the Quakers, who, back in England, were looked upon as the religious fanatics of their time.

About the only aristocrats among the earlier settlers were the younger sons, the poor relations, and the black sheep of the European gentry. But they were in the minority, and the American wilderness showed no favors.

The trading companies spent large sums to collect the colonists and ship them to America. Anticipating big profits, they promised to follow through with ample supplies. But voyages from England were infrequent; and as often as not, the supplies didn't arrive until a year later — along with a letter confidently demanding the first installment of profits.

The settlers couldn't depend on the trading companies,

and the trading companies couldn't depend on the settlers. They wouldn't work. They didn't send the expected furs, and the bond servants frequently skipped out to live with the Indians.

The gentlemen adventurers who had staked their fortunes were righteously indignant. Howling in increasing anguish for the large profits — or for some profits — or at least for the recovery of their cash outlay — they finally wrote it off as a bad investment, and the early trading companies went broke. The colonists were left stranded between an empty sea and an unknown wilderness — both totally indifferent to their fate.

Work or Starve

These were times when even a gentleman had to work — or starve. No one of the aristocratic class had ever faced such a choice. And those of the lower classes were in an even worse predicament. They had always depended on someone else to provide them with jobs. But on this side of the world, jobs didn't exist. They had to create their own jobs. They had to use their heads as well as their hands. It was either that or starve.

They were up against stern reality, and no one could afford the illusion that anything other than his own will controlled his productive powers. Each came to realize that the only source of wealth is human energy attacking this earth; that he alone was responsible for his life; that if he didn't save it, nothing would.

Thus, the slipshod practices of the early trading companies served to plant the seeds of self-reliance. From the very beginning, it was "root hog or die"; and in the desperate effort to survive, they were learning how to wrest a pretty good living from the American wilderness.

Reports going back to England became a bit more favorable, and some of the gentlemen adventurers who had managed to get permits began to flirt with the idea of taking up residence in the New World.

As early as 1630, John Winthrop of the Massachusetts Bay Company moved to America, along with the settlers who founded the town of Ipswich, Massachusetts. When King Charles heard about this, he was quite shocked — particularly when he learned that Governor Winthrop had taken the charter along with him, instead of leaving it safely deposited at the London headquarters, as was customary.

From then on, the absentee-landlord proposition began to wane. The idea of winning fame and fortune in the New World had a strong appeal to some of the more adventuresome men of means.

The Calverts

There was George Calvert, the first Lord Baltimore, who was granted a patent to the Chesapeake Bay region. After his death, this land was colonized under the direction of his son.

The Calverts were Roman Catholics; and while their major aim was to make money, they were also interested in providing a refuge for others of their faith. There was considerable resentment on the part of the earlier colonists. They still harbored the Old World prejudices and didn't relish the idea of Catholics gaining a foothold in the New World.

But in spite of this, or perhaps because of it, the Calverts from first to last set an example of liberalism, religious tolerance, live and let live, which is reflected even to this day in the admirable traditions of the Maryland Free State.

The Quakers

There was young William Penn, the son of a British admiral, who became a Quaker, much to the disgust of his distinguished father. He was a rebel at heart and refused to remove his hat in the presence of the King, but he managed to get a land grant in payment of a debt which the Crown owed his estate.

Accompanied by a hundred fellow-Quakers, Penn moved to America in the year 1682. Again the reception was none too cordial. Pacifism had no place on the rugged frontier, and the Quaker doctrines didn't jibe with those of the Puritans. But Penn, too, ran things on a liberal basis, with major emphasis on industry and thrift rather than on religion.

Incidentally, he was America's first great advertiser. He deluged Europe with promotional material extolling the virtues of Pennsylvania, and he offered special inducements to prospective settlers who were able to help finance themselves. But he held out no false promises of easy riches. First, last, and always, his emphasis was on opportunity through hard work.

It was Penn, perhaps more than anyone else, who started the influx of the great European middle classes — especially the sturdy and industrious Germans. According to David Muzzey:

"William Penn was the greatest of the founders of the American colonies. He had all the liberality of Roger Williams without his impatience, all the fervor of John Winthrop without a trace of intolerance, and all the tact of Lord Baltimore with still greater industry and zeal."[11]

The success of these early pioneers was doubtlessly responsible for attracting others from the aristocratic classes, and the English law of primogeniture was not without its influence. The eldest son inherited his father's estate and title; the younger sons were left to shift for themselves — and America was coming to be recognized as the land of opportunity.

The Cavaliers

The migration to the New World was accelerated by the inquisitions of Cromwell, under which the Cavaliers found it uncomfortable and even dangerous to remain in England. They fled to America for reasons not dissimilar to those which, a century earlier, had prompted the young Conquistadors to follow Cortes and Balboa.

Contrary to the general impression, the word *cavalier* is not synonymous with *aristocracy*. It was merely the name of the political party which supported Charles I and which included many people of humble origin.

The Cavaliers were temperamental, romantic individualists, and they made an effective complement to the Puritans and Quakers. Henry Woodfin Grady summed it up most admirably when in the interest of "preserving a sort of historical equilibrium," he reminded a New England audience that the Cavalier, as well as the Puritan, was among the early settlers and that he was "up and able to be about."*

He pointed out that it was the Virginia Cavalier who first challenged France on this continent; that it was John Smith, a Cavalier, who gave New England its very name; that while Miles Standish was cutting off men's ears for courting a girl without her parents' consent and forbidding men to kiss their wives on the Sabbath Day, the intrepid Cavalier was courting and kissing everything in sight; and that the Almighty had vouchsafed great increase to the Cavalier colonies, the huts in the wilderness being as full as the nests in the woods.

I'd like to devote more space to the Virginia Cavalier; but – again paraphrasing Henry Grady – we'll leave him to work out his own salvation, as he has always been able to do with engaging gallantry and charm.

The main point is that from the very beginning, America was the great melting pot. Neither Puritan, Cavalier, nor Quaker long survived as such. But happily, the virtues and customs of each still live to inspire their sons and to preserve the old traditions.

Although most of the Cavaliers settled in Virginia and Maryland, many of them migrated southward. The Caro-

*These quotes and near-quotes are from The New South – a speech delivered before the New England Club in the City of New York, December 21, 1886, by Henry W. Grady – journalist, editor, orator, scholar, ambassador of good-will, self-reliant individualist, and southern gentleman. He is not related to me; but I was born just after his death, and, like thousands of others, I was given his name. Incidentally, The New South is well worth reading as bearing on the problems of today.

Henry Woodfin Grady, The New South and Other Addresses (New York: Charles E. Merrill, 1904), p. 25.

lina region was successfully colonized in the 1650's by people who moved down from Virginia and Pennsylvania. Specializing in turpentine and tar, they got along splendidly until, some 20 years later, a carefully planned colonization effort was launched from England.

A group of highly respected lords, aided and abetted by experts in statecraft, were given a special charter which would make the Carolinas a separate colony. This colony would be set up as a "grand model" of the ideal political structure and would include all the complexities of European feudalism — plus a touch of Plato. In fact, it was so elaborate that the persons required to carry out the theories would be almost as numerous as those left to do the productive work.

The attempts to put the plan into effect resulted in chaos and dissension amounting to open rebellion. Progress was at a standstill until the early 1700's, when the "lord proprietors" passed out of the picture and the Carolinas were set up as two separate colonies. From then on, they were left pretty much in charge of their own affairs, and they grew and prospered.

But theoretical planners never seem to benefit from the lessons of history nor from the failures of their contemporaries. Barely had the Carolinas been restored to a reasonably practical basis of operation, when an even more fantastic plan was launched for the colonization of the last of the 13 colonies.

Enigmatic Edward

The early story of Georgia is the story of just one man. He was James Edward Oglethorpe, a most fascinating, intriguing, imaginative, and lovable personality. Indeed, it would put a strain on the thesaurus to find adjectives that would do him full justice. He was handsome, curly-haired, fastidiously clad, dashing, gallant, debonair, born to the aristocracy, a man of wealth, a fearless and distinguished soldier, an able strategist — and along with all this he was the most unselfish, generous, and noble-minded person to play an important role in colonizing America.

Although head of Britain's most prosperous slave trading corporation, Oglethorpe was a humanitarian at heart. His heart was as big as all outdoors, and his desire to do good to his fellow man overshadowed all of his other interests.

After a few years' schooling at Oxford, he served with the great soldier, Prince Eugene, in the war against the Turks, following which he returned to England and took over his ancestral estate on the banks of the winding river Wey.

A few years later, he was elected to Parliament, and from then on he devoted the greatest part of his life to a wide range of social reforms. He wanted to give the soldiers and sailors a better deal. He was worried about the price of coal. He wanted to provide refuge and relief for the persecuted Protestants of Europe. He spearheaded the agitation for English prison reforms and fought to abolish the stupid law under which decent and industrious people could be thrown into jail for small debts.

A man of great energy and action, Oglethorpe worked day and night — making speeches, writing letters, and publishing tracts at his own expense. He also found time to keep himself posted on colonial affairs and was quite disturbed at the slipshod way in which the colonies were being run.

England's foothold on the American continent was none too secure. Unfriendly Spain was strongly entrenched to the south, and the French were to the west and north. In order for England to hold her own against encroachment, there had to be a better co-ordination of defensive strategy.

Ingenious Plan

It was Oglethorpe's interest in this latter problem which led to a most ingenious and appealing plan — a plan that would not only provide broad opportunities for social reform, but would greatly strengthen the Empire from a military and economic standpoint. His comprehensive proposal added up about as follows:

1. It was not only unjust, but it was also economically wasteful to keep people in prison for small debts. Why not set them up in the New World and at the same time provide a haven for the oppressed Protestants of Europe?

2. There was a vast area of desirable land lying between the Altamaha and Savannah rivers, south of the Carolinas and north of Spanish Florida.

3. Its latitudinal position corresponded to that of China, Persia, Palestine, and the Madeiras, upon whom England was dependent for such important products as silk, hemp, wine, olive oil, spices, and drugs.

4. With proper supervision, such things could doubt-

lessly be produced in the proposed new colony, thus making England independent of foreign sources.

5. By concentrating on such products, the new colony would not in any way conflict with the activities of other colonies.

6. From a military standpoint, it would serve as a buffer between the Carolinas and Spanish Florida. To insure a strong army, special concessions would be made to soldiers — only able-bodied fighting men would be permitted to own land.

7. In the interest of the common good, everything would be beneficently administered under a well-balanced plan. This would not only provide for the necessities of military regimentation, but it would also eliminate the disorders, maladjustments, and wastes of competition.

8. The social aspects would also be carefully supervised. Slaves, rum, and Roman Catholics would be strictly prohibited.

9. The new colony would be named for King George II; and it would be an honor and a credit to him — something to which he could point with pride as an example worthy of emulation by all the other colonies.

10. First, last, and always, Georgia would be a strictly eleemosynary proposition. To avoid dissension and to insure adherence to the high objectives, no one would be allowed to vote. Oglethorpe would look after everything personally, and his motto would be *Non Sibi, Sed Aliis* — Not for Self, but for Others.

Without Argument

This comprehensive proposal was accepted without argument. Not only was the charter granted, but also the English government departed from its usual policy and made a cash contribution of £10,000 to help get things started. Oglethorpe put up some of his own money; and overwhelmed by his logic and persuasiveness, benevolent societies and right-thinking citizens made liberal donations.

With his carefully selected band of settlers, Oglethorpe came to the New World and founded the city of Savannah in the year 1733. From a military standpoint, the project was a success. With a handful of well-trained troops, Oglethorpe not only licked the invading Spaniards, but also took advantage of the opportunity to extend the borders of Georgia considerably southward.

You can read about it in the history books, and it's a most thrilling story. But as I said before, the historians are inclined to stress the war aspects and overlook the lessons that might be learned as bearing on the problems of peace and progress.

Reasons for Failure

In spite of his self-sacrifice and high motives, Oglethorpe's venture was a miserable failure from an economic and sociological standpoint. He failed to recognize that military regimentation always works at cross-purposes to creative progress — that human initiative doesn't operate according to the pattern of a beehive. And incidentally, he overlooked the fact that variations in climate and soil are not wholly dependent on latitude; that regardless of the needs of man-made empires, the Almighty never intended that Georgia should be a substitute for the Orient.

During 20 years of futile effort, the population never exceeded 6,000; and when it dwindled back down to around 500, Oglethorpe gave up in despair and returned to England.

A few years later, all the bans and prohibitions were lifted. The pendulum swung the other way. Things were thrown wide open. "Refugees" who had fled to the Carolinas came back and brought their friends with them, and there was an influx of new blood from Virginia — including the cavalier Talbots. The last of the 13 colonies grew by leaps and bounds; and by the end of the century, its population had passed the 160,000 mark.

Oglethorpe's effort to set up a Utopia was one of the more extreme attempts at regimentation; but it is typical, in many respects, of the type of thing that laid the groundwork for the revolution that was to come.

Chapter 13

ROOTS OF REVOLUTION

THE American rebellion against economic tyranny really had its beginning in the 1660's — about 40 years after the Pilgrims first set foot on New England's coast. This was during the period when England was "a piece of land entirely surrounded by smugglers," and ghouls were digging up London's dead to salvage the woolen shrouds. To improve the industry of his realm, Charles II signed an act permitting the American colonists to ship cotton, lumber, tobacco, and other products to England — but only to England.

It was true that such products were needed in England — most of them were already going there — but it was also true that the colonists needed sugar and molasses from the West Indies. The early Americans were realists. They were fighting the earth and the sea for their lives — and incidentally, they were laying the groundwork for a prosperous trade. The King's seal on a piece of parchment from faraway London didn't impress them, so they kept right on swapping their wool and tobacco for Cuban molasses.

Nothing much came of it. Charles II was a negligent ruler, and he had other problems on his mind (see *Forever Amber*). True, his ships sank a few of the traders' ships, but not one colonist was burned at the stake or even hanged. Running the blockade became an ordinary business risk, and things went along smoothly for almost three-quarters of a century.

Then in 1733, the British government announced a "five-year plan" in order to meet an emergency. The French government was indirectly responsible. In the interest of price maintenance, the French colonists in the West Indies had been prohibited from shipping food to France. The result was overproduction, and the desperate islanders were ready to sell their products for anything they could get.

The British government, to protect its subjects against this low-priced competition, ordered the colonists to stop trading with the French West Indies. But the Americans had different ideas. Traffic in molasses, sugar, and rum had become the backbone of their business. Their prosperity depended on the West Indies trade. To cut it off would mean a serious depression — and why shouldn't they take advantage of the lower prices?

An Emergency Measure

American businessmen decided that it was time to have a showdown. They were trying to build a new country; and it was a tough job, even without such artificial interference with the natural and normal flow of trade. They tried to explain the facts back in London; but after two years of "careful consideration," the British government soothingly replied that it was only an "emergency measure" — it might hurt a little at first but after another three years the law would automatically expire, and everyone would be better off.

But the colonists didn't quite see it that way, and many

who had never broken a law took occasion to indulge in a little temporary smuggling.

At the end of the five-year period, apparently the emergency wasn't quite over, so the British government renewed the Molasses Act — again assuring the colonists that it was only a temporary measure, just an extension of the "five-year plan" for another five years.

By this time, conditions in America paralleled the prohibition era of the 1920's. People were losing respect for legal authority. The law was a joke, and everyone enjoyed breaking it. Each home had its contraband jug of molasses, its sugar loaf, its rum toddy, its rum tea, and its buttered rum.

In and out of the ports and along the coast and across the Caribbean, the agile trading ships showed their heels to His Majesty's Navy — or, when cornered, they stood and fought, cheered on by the folks back home.

Trade was on the boom. Visitors from Europe marveled at the prosperity. And in 1748, the reliable British government, still coping with the "temporary emergency," renewed the Molasses Act — and business went on as usual for another five years.

Off and on for almost a century, running the blockade had been just one of the ordinary risks of doing business. Of course, the King's gunners added to the overhead and kept prices a bit higher than they should have been — but that was all. America continued to grow and prosper. By this time, the British colonies were almost as old as the United States is today. They were no longer frontier settlements. Four generations of self-reliant settlers had established towns and farms which were more productive than any in Europe.

Franklin, Washington, and Patrick Henry

Ben Franklin, the self-educated young radical from Boston, had moved to Philadelphia and was building up his own printing business from scratch. George Washington, in his teens, was carrying a musket and keeping a sharp lookout for Indians while earning his living as a surveyor in the Virginia wilderness. Patrick Henry, after going broke — first as a storekeeper and then as a farmer — had now taken up the study of law.

Along the Mississippi, the Ohio, the James, the Delaware, and the Hudson, such men read Voltaire, Rousseau, Montesquieu, and Locke. But among the uncultured farmers, sailors, hunters, and trappers, reading was limited to almanacs, small-town papers, and, more than anything else, the Bible.

Most of the colonists remembered grandfathers, even fathers, who had risked their lives to read the Bible. They knew of men who had been burned at the stake, wrenched joint from joint on the rack, broken on the wheel for saying — or even for being accused of saying — that ordinary men had a right to read the Bible. They had heard old people talk of stealthy meetings at night to hear the Bible read in secret by the light of a shaded candle — of the alarm, the terror, the frantic escapes. They'd been told of meetings back on the open moors of Scotland, where people gathered to recite the Scriptures under a moonless sky — of the sudden "Halloo," the charging horses, and the frantic running before the galloping troopers, who rode down men and women and slashed at them with swords; then the long period of hiding while the troopers searched craftily and wives of slain men lay under water in the ditches, praying to God that their babies would not whimper and that the hunt might end before dawn.

The children of such people were happy to be in a land where they could fearlessly read their Bibles. They read about adventures and crimes, of hairbreadth escapes, of wars and spies, of political intrigues, of shepherds and vineyards and business deals, and of young lovers and family life.

And when they read the words of Abraham, Moses, Christ, and all the prophets, who said that men are self-controlling and responsible, it checked with their experience; and they knew it was true. They could have told similar stories of their own lives, if the words had only come to mind.

Modernized Pagans

The colonists had never believed in the ancient pagan gods, and few of them had even heard of the modern pagan gods which were then being created by the Old World intellectuals.

The Age of Science was dawning. It could no longer be denied that the earth is round and spinning in space. Intrepid individualists were prying into the secrets of nature. Galvani had captured something tingling in a jar. Ben Franklin had pulled the same sort of thing out of the sky on a kite string and had proved that it was lightning.

The Old World philosophers recovered from the shock of these new ideas — but they did not give up their pagan superstitions. They concluded that there is no God and

[169]

then proceeded with great ingenuity to make a god of science.

They recognized natural law but narrowed its meaning to exclude the possibility of progress. They explained that everything is controlled by physical force. Man's emotions, sentiments, imagination, and creative urges have no place in the picture. The universe is a giant mechanism. Its wheels revolve forever. Everything is foreordained. There is no will. There is no high spiritual purpose — no divine plan. Nothing is created. There is no Creator.

Man is unimportant, they said. As an individual, he counts for nought. He is but an insignificant animal among many species of animals — no more than dust on the cogs of the giant mechanism.

"But," one may well ask, "what controls the controls?"

The answer is *natural law*. At least, that was the answer of the French intellectuals who were leading the people of Europe back to the era of pre-Christian thought. They said that natural law controls everything, including man — except that civilization had somehow got the upper hand. Civilization is an unnatural control; it causes all human miseries. And since religion is the basis of civilization, science must make war against religion — religion must be destroyed.

The Enlightened Despot

After the evils of civilization and religion are wiped out, an "enlightened despot" will establish the Age of Reason, based on natural law. When that has been accomplished, the enlightened despot will "wither away," and natural man — at last living naturally — will be good and happy ever after.

That, as nearly as I can understand, is what the great European intellectuals seem to have believed. And they lived on the bounty of the aristocrats while writing their books and plays designed to destroy the aristocracy and thus to clear the way for the enlightened despot who would run things according to their learned theories.

It seems that most of them were betting on Prussia's Frederick the Great who was responsible for the Seven Years' War — which, according to his boastful claim, he had started on a whim.

Frederick was an ardent atheist and an able schemer. He greatly admired the French intellectuals, and they were favored guests at his court. Their theories fitted in with his dreams for a new world empire — with Frederick, of course, as the enlightened despot.

England was now under the rule of her second German king; and as an ally of Prussia, she had turned her guns on France. Quaintly enough, the colonists called it the "French and Indian War."

On this side of the Atlantic, both governments were seeking allies among the Indians. Both sides bribed them with firewater. Both sides armed them with weapons. Both sides paid liberally for scalps. So the Red Men set fire to the White Men's cabins. Settlers on both sides were scalped or burned at the stake. Their wives were taken as squaws, and their children grew up as Indians.

The Old World quarrels had extended to the New World. Along the outlying frontiers, things were very bad. And along the Atlantic coast, business was at a standstill.

Bright Idea

But self-preservation is the first law of nature. People must eat; trade must go on.

Out of the war itself, the resourceful colonists devised a peaceful way of doing business, and it was a bright idea: Governments at war have prisoners to exchange. Why couldn't traders exchange the prisoners?

So they bribed the British and French officials and obtained permits to sail the seas and to exchange the prisoners. As long as the great powers continued to fight, businessmen on both sides carried on a prosperous trade with each other. Their ships no longer ran from their governments' navies. A captain would merely stand to, wait for the King's officers to come aboard, and meet them with a smile — and a permit.

A lively business in these permits developed at every port. The permits were sold at public auction — prices depended on supply and demand, and speculators on the sidelines played the "permit market."

Trading was peaceful, and business boomed until the war came to an end in 1763.

There were no more prisoners to exchange, but the Molasses Act was again renewed as an emergency measure. The American traders put the guns back on their ships and began to readjust their activities to a peacetime basis.

The Next Best Bet

Back in London, the British government was undergoing a change. George II had died in the middle of the war, and his grandson had come to the throne in 1760. George William Frederick was the third of the Hanoverian line of rulers who had been brought over from Germany in 1714, after the House of Stuarts had run its course. The first two Georges had been rather prone to take things easy. They hadn't even bothered to learn the English language and had depended largely on their ministers to run things.

With George III, it was going to be different. He was only twenty-two years old when he came to the throne, but he was a hard worker and a stickler for detail. For the first time in generations, England had a conscientious ruler. In common with his cousin, Frederick the Great, young George was an ardent admirer of the European intellectuals, who were still looking for an enlightened despot to put their theories into effect.

Frederick the Great was losing interest. He was too busy with domestic affairs to worry about a world empire, and rumor had it that he was becoming a bit too tolerant towards the Christian religion. George III looked like the next best bet.

Time and circumstances offered big opportunities for the new king. England had been too loosely governed. The planning had been inadequate. For too long, the colonists had been flouting the authority of the Crown. Something must be done, and George III was the man to do it. Spurred on by an ambitious mother, he intended to bring to the English people the benefits of law and order — with systematic regimentation in the best Prussian manner.

As soon as the war was over, the young monarch rose to the occasion and earnestly set about the job of working out every detail affecting the lives of his subjects, at home and abroad. And truly, no living authority ever could have planned an economy with greater thoroughness.

Thoughtful Planning

Aided and abetted by his statisticians, he became alarmed at the growth of the colonies, which, according to statistics, threatened to depopulate the British Isles and to make a ghost town of London within another 50 years.

George III took immediate action to prevent the impending catastrophe. First, he restricted emigration to the colonies. Then, to further retard their expansion, he prohibited any more settlers from moving westward. In the interest of protecting the future of the fur trade, the area from the Alleghenies to the Mississippi was forever reserved for the Indians.*

But given the facts as they were at the time, no one could have planned an economy more wisely than did young King George. With his "brain trust" at his elbow and with the welfare of his subjects always of primary concern, he balanced everything most admirably. Agriculture was in the colonies; industry, in England. He set about to regulate both and to provide British shipping with the triangular voyage between England, the American ports, and the West Indies.

This home-office planning was extended to include even the American trees. The King's men went through

---

*It is interesting to note that the pioneer fur traders in their greatest days never got from the Mississippi Valley more than a sixth of the valuable furs it now produces.

the forests, marking the best pines to be held in reserve for the royal Navy. This thoughtful prudence so irritated the colonists that they went out of their way to use these pines for themselves. Then, adding insult to injury, they adopted the pine tree as their symbol of liberty. In later years, it was displayed on the flags flying from the masts of American fighting ships during the first war of the revolution.

The Common Good

It is unfair to place too much blame on George III. He did everything conscientiously and in the interest of what he conceived to be the "common good." But down through the years, the colonists had grown tired of being the pawns of Old World bureaucracy. They were fed up with all the rules and red tape which interfered with the normal, natural job of applying their energies to the production of goods and services. Things had reached a point where they had lost all sense of distinction between good laws and bad laws.

The Old World mind couldn't understand this. Why, for instance, should the colonists object to the Stamp Tax? A small, suitable tax on legal documents should not be a burden to anyone. But the colonists refused to pay, and the law was repealed.

And who could explain the Boston Tea Party? There had been an overproduction of tea. The East India Trading Company needed protection. If something were not done, the price of tea would fall, and the tea growers of India would suffer a depression. To prevent this disaster, the British government might have burned the surplus —

just as the Brazilian government once ordered the burning of coffee, and just as our own "brain trusters" ordered the killing of little pigs. But King George was more sensible. He had the tea shipped to the American colonies at a controlled price — a little less than they had been paying, a little more than a free market would have supported.*

Did the colonists applaud this wise measure for the good of all? They did not — they raided the ship and threw the tea into Boston Harbor.

The Boston Tea Party

This act of violence and willful destruction of property was immediately condemned by leading patriots, including Benjamin Franklin and John Adams.

The incident would doubtlessly have been smoothed over, except that King George and his bureaucrats unwittingly came to the aid of the rioters. The port of Boston was ordered closed to all outside commerce. The Massachusetts charter was revoked. One of the King's military henchmen was appointed governor and was given sweeping administrative powers. Town meetings were prohibited. Persons accused of resisting law enforcement were to be deported to England for trial. Last, but not least — and the thing that was most irritating to the Puritans — the boundaries of the province of Quebec were extended to include everything north of the Ohio River.

---

*It is the invariable intent of all economic regulations to prevent a fall in prices, at any cost. Actually, of course, lower prices increase consumption and production and trade and jobs.

[176]

The Boston Tea Party is usually thought of as the beginning of the American Revolution; but for more than a century, the colonists had been rebelling against the tyranny of Old World monarchs. From the early 1660's to the surrender of Cornwallis at Yorktown, they had continuously revolted against just one thing — authority presuming to control the initiative and creative energy of human beings. Five hundred men had come out of the frontier cabins in Virginia to oust the royal Governor, who protected the graft-paying sale of guns and whiskey to the Indians. In the Carolinas, in Pennsylvania, in Connecticut, in Massachusetts, in the New Hampshire grants, and on the high seas, their rebellion had been continuous and increasing.

At last, the British government was compelled to use the only power that any state has at its disposal — the power of brute force used with general consent. But when the King's troops were moved into Boston to take things over, the Americans did not consent. They stood their ground as free individuals, and they fought the British Regulars.

Without a Leader

The great fact in history is this: *The American Revolution had no leader*. This fact is the hope of the world because human freedom is a personal matter. Only the individual can protect human rights in the infinite complexity of men's relationships with each other. Nothing on earth is more valuable than the person who knows that all men are free and who accepts the responsibilities that go with freedom.

The pioneer Americans knew that they were free. They had learned it the hard way—from stern experience. So when the British government tried to regiment them and obstruct their efforts, they simply ignored it. When the King laid down silly restrictions and controls on trade, the colonists went right on trading. When the weaving of cloth was prohibited in order to protect weavers in England, the women of America kept right on working at their looms.

Chapter 14

THE UNKNOWN INDIVIDUAL

THE war for American independence was begun by an individual. He was asleep in his bed when someone pounded on his door and shouted out in the night: "The Redcoats are coming!"

But what could he do? He was only one man against the armed might of Britain. If he had been a king, a czar, or a potentate, he could have solved vast problems and done great things — he could have brought the powers of Europe together in harmony and made an everlasting peace and prosperity around the world.

But he was not a king, not a royal governor, not a rich man, not an important man. He was just one little man, unknown to anyone outside of his own neighborhood. So what could he do? Why should he take the initiative? Such things usually cleared up — they always had. So why not let nature take its course? This was no time to be foolhardy. He must keep calm, use his head, and consider the practical aspects. And there was his family to think of. What would become of them?

Most men felt that way. They knew they could do nothing, and they had better sense than to try. That night in Lexington, many of them stayed in bed. But the unknown individual chose between submission that looked like safety and rebellion that seemed utterly hopeless. Many respected citizens were against him; the teachers and the writers of books were against him. Men in high places — many widely-known men — stood stanchly with the King.

But the unknown individual had the courage of his convictions. He got up, put on his clothes, took his gun, and went out to meet the British troops. Not acting under orders, not being led nor wanting to be the leader, he stood on his own feet — a responsible, self-controlling person — and fired the shot heard 'round the world. The sound of that shot said that man is a free agent; that government is the servant rather than the master.

Ebenezer Fox

The records are scant. The unknown man had no biographer. He was just a plain, ordinary person who had learned from his own experience that each human being is self-controlling — responsible for his own acts and for his relations with others.

Ebenezer Fox was such a man, and he typifies thousands of Americans of his time. Ebenezer helped fight the War for Independence as an ordinary seaman under the pine-tree flag; and in the early 1800's, he wrote down his "simple narrative" for his grandchildren because, he said, they liked to hear him tell it.[12]

He was born in the East Parish of Roxbury, Massachusetts in January, 1763. His father, a tailor, was a poor man with a large family; so Ebenezer at the age of seven was signed over to a farmer named Pelham. This was not unusual. In those days, most families expected a boy of seven to be self-supporting, either at home or as a servant to someone else. It sounds a bit shocking; but as

[180]

Mrs. Lane points out, this same thinking still prevails in eastern Europe and western Asia. Even in the United States, as late as the 1860's, the age of self-support was only nine.

Suffering many hardships and privations, Ebenezer frequently complained to his father, but the elder Fox paid no attention to his son's grievances. He assumed that they arose merely from a spirit of discontent and would soon subside.

In the meantime, Ebenezer was hearing considerable talk about the tyranny of government and "Expressions of exasperated feeling against the government of Great Britain . . . from the mouths of all classes. . . ."

He pondered over the things he heard and began to apply them to his own circumstances: "I thought that I was doing myself great injustice by remaining in bondage, when I ought to go free; and that the time was come, when I should liberate myself . . . and . . . do what was right in the sight of my own eyes."

So, at the age of twelve, Ebenezer ran away from his master and got a job on a ship going to Santo Domingo. Returning with a contraband cargo of molasses and coffee, the ship was attacked by two British gunboats off Stonington, Connecticut. Young Ebenezer jumped overboard, stripped off his clothes in the water, swam to shore under fire from the British guns, and barely escaped drowning.

Thus he returned from his first voyage, penniless and stark naked — "without injury, but nearly exhausted from fatigue and fear, not a little augmented by the sound of the bullets that whistled around my head while in the water. . . . My appearance among them [the rest of the crew on shore] in a state of entire nakedness excited not a little mirth. . . . But after a few jests at my expense, the mate took off one of the two shirts, with which he had taken the precaution to provide himself before he left the vessel, and gave it to me."

A little later, Ebenezer Fox volunteered to fight for independence. He was wounded, captured, and starved on the British "floating hell" in Long Island Sound; but he escaped and re-enlisted.

He became a gunner, which cost him the hearing in one ear, but he fought through to the end. When the war was over and the American ships had no further need for gunners, Ebenezer, along with other members of his crew, was left stranded in France and had to work his way home as best he could.

Back in those days, there were no veterans' benefits. Ebenezer's pay for five years of hard fighting consisted of his low wages, paid in the almost-worthless Continental currency, and his 30-dollar share of the prize money from a captured British ship.

Such men began and won the War for Independence. For ten years, they had been storming British forts. They came out of their homes and fought at Lexington. In June, they stood against wave after wave of British troops at the Battle of Bunker Hill; but it was not until the following February, when that historic hilltop was white with snow, that they had a leader.

America's Godfather

His name was Thomas Paine. He was a workman, poor and growing old. He had spent most of his childhood helping his father, an English corset maker. But he had managed to get a few years' schooling and had learned to read and write — a rare privilege for a working-class boy. He married a tobacconist's daughter. They inherited her father's tiny shop in Lewes, England. Paine's wife died, and the little shop was sold for debt. He struggled along at various jobs until he was nearly forty; then friends lent him money to pay his passage to America.

Benjamin Franklin gave him a letter to a Philadelphia printer, who hired him at $5.00 a month to start a little publication called the *Pennsylvania Magazine.*

That was in the year 1775. The colonies were blockaded and could get no gunpowder. The new editor launched the first copy of the *Pennsylvania Magazine* with a recipe for homemade gunpowder. It was a sensational success, and Americans, mixing the ingredients in their kitchens, may have noticed the name of the editor — a name, then obscure, which was to resound down through history.

Thomas Paine had taken up writing at middle age; and, in contrast to the pompous style of the 18th century writers, he avoided quoting the classics and wrote in the simple language of the people. He saved his money and printed a little pamphlet covering his views on freedom. The pamphlet bore the title *Common Sense.* It came off the press early in 1776, and in all the history of printing, there has never been such a spontaneous sale. It was not copyrighted; there were no copyright laws, and anyway, Paine wanted no profit from his political writings. The first edition didn't even bear his name. It was widely reprinted; and it has been estimated that, out of a population of 3,000,000 people, more than 300,000 bought copies. Translated into present-day terms, that would correspond to a sale of around 14,000,000 copies.

All who could read, read it. Others listened while it was read to them. It said to Americans: Do what is right in your own eyes. Cut loose from England. Set up a government of your own. "We have it in our power to begin the world over again. A situation, similar to the present, hath not happened since the days of Noah until now."[13]

Shortly thereafter, Paine enlisted as a private in the defeated colonial army, which was falling back before the British advance — from Long Island to Manhattan, across Jersey, across the Delaware, across Pennsylvania. When Congress had taken to its heels and soldiers were deserting and cautious men were hastening to proclaim their loyalty to the King, Thomas Paine, by the light of a campfire, spread a scrap of paper on a drumhead and wrote:

"These are the times that try men's souls. The summer soldier and the sunshine patriot will, in this crisis, shrink from the service of their country; . . . Tyranny, like hell, is not easily conquered; . . . What we obtain too cheap, we esteem too lightly: . . . it would be strange indeed if so celestial an article as FREEDOM should not be highly rated."[13-a]

His ringing words cut through the gloom of defeat. In every colony, courage rose to meet the challenge, and George Washington declared that Thomas Paine was worth more than an entire army. This plain-spoken man was the leader and the spirit of the new revolution. In America, England, and France, he was the greatest political influence of his century.

The Declaration

More than a year after Bunker Hill and six months after Paine's *Common Sense* had raised all the unheard voices into one loud roar for independence, an extraordinary meeting was held in Philadelphia.

It seems that Thomas Jefferson had asked Paine to help draw up a statement reviewing the causes of the war and including a simple declaration of the principle for which the people were fighting. The tentative document was now ready, and representatives from each of the colonies had come to the meeting to consider its adoption.

These representatives were gentlemen of solid responsibility and high social position — including Benjamin Franklin, John Adams, Richard Henry Lee, Charles Carroll, Robert Morris, John Hancock, James Wilson, Roger Sherman, and George Walton. Such men had everything to gain by standing with the King. If they joined the rebels, they risked not only their own lives, but also the lives of their families. Under English law, their children and their children's children would be attainted traitors.

Each man attending the meeting possessed a landed estate, a substantial business, a professional position — or all three. He need only do nothing. By keeping quiet, he might save his property, his superior class status, and his life. And he could easily justify his position on the premise that, while he might not wholly agree with the government's policies, a good subject's duty is to obey the laws and remain loyal to his king.

Some of them refused to sign, and each man who did sign knew what he risked when he wrote his signature under the words: "We mutually pledge to each other our

Lives. . . ." He was prepared to lose his life when he signed a declaration of that ten-year-old war, its causes and its motives:

> "We hold these truths to be self-evident, that all men are created equal, that they are endowed by their Creator with certain unalienable Rights, that among these are Life, Liberty and the pursuit of Happiness."

The Philadelphia group was undertaking not only to win the war, but to lay the groundwork for an entirely new kind of state. They were assuming leadership of the weak and losing side, and the problems were many. First of all, money would have to be raised, and the military effort would have to be better organized. Scattered mobs could never defeat Great Britain.

The prospects were not bright. The King's troops were advancing down the Hudson River. His fleet was approaching New York. The leaders of the Revolution were faced with the armed might of the British Empire — with 13 disorganized and quarreling colonies at their backs.

Dissension

The different colonies had grown up as separate units. They were divided by religion, customs, economic interests, and commercial rivalries. If the war were to be won, they would have to be brought together in a unified objective. And winning the war would mean very little unless a political structure could be devised which would solve the kind of problems that had brought on the war.

Many prominent citizens — landholders, bankers, rich merchants, and speculators — were unmindful of the underlying causes of the Revolution; they were looking forward to the time when America would be set up as a monarchy, independent of Europe, but following the Old World pattern of a living authority. Others were clamoring for an out-and-out democracy, overlooking the fact that down through history all such attempts had led to tyranny and rebellion.

Each of the representatives at Philadelphia knew that men are free, and yet there was a wide difference of viewpoint as to what form of political structure would keep men free.

The Declaration had abolished government, but this was war. The revolutionary leaders must have authority to mobilize, arm, command, and feed the troops; and taxes would have to be collected to pay the bills. But any authority which they might exercise over any other man must be given to them by that man, so it was necessary to call for a general grant of authority from the people in the colonies.

Time and space would not permit all of them to meet in one place; they must meet in many places, and each group must send someone to represent all the individuals in that group.*

From all the colonies, messengers on horseback went galloping through the woods to the secret meeting places

*The idea was not new. For generations past, the colonists in their scattered and unprotected settlements had been getting together in times of danger, sending their representatives to get help — to bargain for it, if necessary — and to make formal agreements with other colonies. So they were used to the idea of delegating to one man their natural right of free speech and free contract. These early beginnings ultimately led to the invention of a new and unique device called the "convention of delegates."

to find out what was happening, to get instructions as to what should be done by the folks back home, and, above all, to make sure that no one tried to set up a central government which would infringe on their rights. Frequently, the King's troops were at the meeting place ahead of the messengers; but amidst alarms, defeats, and retreats, most of the delegates managed to get together.

The State Constitutions

In their spare moments, some of the delegates would take quill in hand and write out substitutes for the royal charters under which their colonies had been operating.

The state constitution was an outgrowth of the royal charter. Each colony had had its own separate charter — based on the Old World belief that an authority controls the individual and that no person can do anything without its permission.

The state constitution would have to be just the reverse of the royal charter. It would have to define the uses of force that would and would not be granted to public officials. It was a matter of turning things upside down, and there was no precedent to serve as a guide.

Able men in every colony — consulting frequently with the representatives of other colonies — continued their efforts to develop state constitutions which would be in harmony with the principles laid down in the Declaration of Independence.

Over and over again, the state constitutions were rewritten; over and over again, they were rejected by the people.

For six long years, the revolutionary leaders tried to

evade the King's troops, to hold the struggling army together, to get food and shoes and powder and bullets from stupid politicians and grafters, who stole the money and would have let the soldiers die. They negotiated loans from France and tried to get French help against the British. While they were doing all these things, they were also trying to persuade Americans to agree to the constitutions.

But the unknown Americans — the Ebenezer Foxes — were fighting authority, and each was determined to do what was right in his own eyes. They were resentful of anything that even resembled authority, and they did not intend to let a new power grow up as fast as they cut the old one down.

Grudgingly and most suspiciously, the colonies, one after another, did agree to their state constitutions — but not until strict prohibitions against the misuse of force had been clearly set forth in each constitution.

Dilemma

Then the people of the different states couldn't make up their minds whether to unite or to become separate nations. If they were to unite in one strong government, what would happen to the freedom for which they were fighting? And there was strenuous argument between the large states and the small states as to how many votes each would be allowed in case they did join the Union.

They realized that their freedom would be endangered if they did not unite. Americans occupied only a small part of the New World. Most of the Western Hemisphere was still in the possession of Britain, France, and Spain.

The heterogeneous and scattered states, weakened under the strain of war, could hardly hope to survive unless united under some kind of centralized government strong enough to hold its own against the great powers of the world.

Chapter 15

THE NEW MODEL

ANOTHER six years of confusion and discouragement followed the surrender of Cornwallis. The leaders of the Revolution were negotiating the peace treaty and trying to hold the Continental Congress together, to keep the states from fighting each other, and to figure out a way to pay something on the French debt before the French army moved in to collect it. During this period, when George Washington had less hope than at Valley Forge, the leaders of the Revolution made one last effort to unite the independent states.

With the state constitutions as their guide, they attempted to write an over-all constitution which would combine the states into a co-operative federation, designed to work on the principles of individual freedom, liberty, and law.

Common men were to run their own affairs. All persons were to have equal power so that each would be free to struggle for his own self-interest, in order to arrive at a satisfactory balance in his relationships with other men.

The problem was not new. It was as old as history, but no one had ever found the answer. The Greeks had been unable to solve it. The Romans had been unable to solve it. Various experiments had been tried, and all had failed.

No one had ever found the solution. But it is doubtful

that, in the entire history of mankind, so unusual a group had ever come together for so important a purpose — realistic frontiersmen, practical builders, jurists, statesmen, students of history, analysts of Old World government from the perspective of a New World in the making. Their counterparts are rare in this modern age of specialization and so-called "progressive" education.[*]

Democracy was not the answer. The word *democracy* means rule by the masses, and mass rule means mob rule. As James Madison pointed out in *The Federalist*:

"A pure democracy . . . can admit of no cure for the mischiefs of faction. A common passion or interest will . . . be felt by a majority . . . and there is nothing to check the inducements to sacrifice the weaker party. . . . Hence it is that such democracies have ever been . . . found incompatible with personal security or the rights of property; and have in general been as short in their lives as they have been violent in their death."

Obviously, there can be no individual freedom unless the rights of the minority are protected; and in an unrestrained democracy, it's too easy for the organized pressure groups to infringe on the rights of others.

[*]To be fitted for public office in later life, it was then considered necessary for a boy to be given the education of an English gentleman. Before he was sixteen, the philosophy and history of the entire European past had been pounded into his head. Thus, when he was old enough to begin thinking things out for himself, he had within his own mind a storehouse of knowledge covering thousands of years of human experience. Also, he was drilled in logic and the accurate meaning of words, as essential to straight-thinking and as a protection against the fallacies of fancy rhetoric! (One of these days, I hope to write a book, or at least a pamphlet, on the educational techniques that produced such men as Washington, Jefferson, and Madison — with a special chapter on the Donald Robertson School.)

A Republic

America was to be set up as a republic — which means that the laws would be made and administered by representatives chosen, directly or indirectly, by the people to protect the interests of *all* the people.

The word *republic* means rule *for* the people, and as Isabel Paterson points out:

> "A Republic signifies an organization dealing with affairs which concern the public, thus implying that there are also private affairs, a sphere of social and personal life, with which government is not and should not be concerned; it sets a limit to the political power."[1-a]

In the last analysis, any government, regardless of what it may be called, must be one man or a small group of men in power over many men. That being the case, how is it possible to transfer the power of the ruler to each man in the multitude?

The answer is that it is not possible. The only solution lies in the direction of destroying power itself. The only way in which men can remain free and be left in control of their individual energies is to cut the power of government to an irreducible minimum.

But how can that be done without the danger of out-and-out anarchy? The answer is quite simple — once it is found. But until the time of the American Revolution, no one had found it.

The head of a state is a human being; and a human being's thinking, deciding, acting, and judging are inseparable. But in this new American republic, no top official

would ever be permitted to act as a whole human being.
The functions of government would be divided into three
parts:

1. The first part was to think and decide. It would be
   called the *Congress*.
2. The second part was to be responsible for getting
   action. It would be headed by the chief executive
   — the *President*.
3. The third part was to serve as judge or referee and
   would be known as the *Supreme Court*.

Each of these three parts was to act as a check on the
the other two; and over the three was set a written statement of political principles, intended to be the strongest
check on them all. There was to be government by law —
with clearly defined rules of the game — rather than government by whim. Thus, the Constitution was to serve as
an impersonal restraint upon the fallible human beings
who must be allowed to use their fragments of authority
over the multitudes of free individuals.

The dangers of dictatorship must be avoided for all
time to come. No one person nor small group of persons
must ever be permitted to get too much power; and the
minority — even down to the last individual citizen —
must be protected against oppression by the majority or
by any organized pressure group.

Such were the objectives of the American revolutionary leaders, and for months they struggled to draw the
blueprints for this new and completely different political
structure.

Then they went out and fought for two more years in
an effort to get it accepted. With arguments and speeches,

with pamphlets and newspapers and books, with appeals to logic and justice and common sense and self-interest, with political deals — with every weapon they had — they fought the demand for monarchy, and they fought the demand for democracy.

The war ended on October 19, 1781. The peace was formally ratified September 3, 1783. But the United States did not come into being until June, 1788, at which time the federal Constitution had been accepted by nine states — but only on the condition that it be amended to include certain specific restrictions and reservations to protect the individual against the improper use of force, and to prevent the central government from encroaching on the rights of the state governments.

Servant, Not Master

In effect, the Ebenezer Foxes said to the revolutionary leaders: "We don't mind joining in a voluntary federation, with a limited organization to look after the overall problems. But we are not as much interested in the good things that you *could* do as we are in the bad things that you or your successors *might* do if there were too much centralized power. It should be clearly understood, once and for all, that we don't propose to drift back into the same sort of situation which brought on the war. We want no European regimentation on this side of the world!

"The whole idea is to protect the freedom of the individual citizen, not only from outsiders, but from insiders — and especially from men in public office. All up and down the line, it's got to be government by law, not government by violence. Things must be run according to the rules of the game, not by the whims and fancies of those whom we elect to office. There is no one person nor small group of persons smart enough to run this country — even if we, the citizens, were smart enough to pick the best of the lot.

"The federal government, along with state governments, county governments, and city governments, must be set up as the servant rather than as the master — and it must be kept that way.

"We're the ones who will have to put up the money, and *we* will write the ticket. It's your job to preserve law and order so that we can be free to get our work done. That's why we are giving you a monopoly of the use of force. We are giving it voluntarily, and it is not to be used in a manner that will interfere with the constructive activities of free citizens."

The first ten amendments were the "price of ratification." They guarantee freedom of speech, freedom of the press, religious freedom, and the right of trial by jury. In addition, public officials are forbidden to seize or to search a person or his property or his private papers — except under certain definite circumstances prescribed by written law. Private property cannot be taken for public use without just compensation to its owner.* Cruelty is

*For the first time in history, the right to own property was to be given full legal recognition and was to be extended to the humblest citizen, without reference to class distinction, social position, or status of birth. The moral right of private ownership had long been recognized by the Christian Church as essential to spiritual freedom. But outside the Church, the idea had gained little headway. As late as 1776, for example, no one in France could own even so much as a pigeon, unless he happened to be a person of "royal birth" — a king, a prince, or a noble.

outlawed once and for all, and any accused person is to be considered innocent until his guilt is proven.

And last, but not least, it became a part of constitutional law that any powers not specifically granted to the Federation automatically remain in the hands of the separate states or in the hands of the people themselves.

Thus, the individual's life, liberty, and property rights are to be held secure against unjust acts, not only on the part of other individuals, but also on the part of the government itself.

A Misleading Term

These early amendments are known collectively as the "Bill of Rights," but the name is misleading and tends to confuse a careless mind.

The word *rights* reflects the feudal concept. It is entirely accurate as used in England because the English "bill of rights" is a statement of certain freedoms which the British government *permits* its subjects.

But in America, it's exactly the opposite. Our so-called Bill of Rights is really a statement of prohibitions, and it defines the uses of force that will or will not be granted to public officials. It is based on the principle that human rights are natural rights — born in every human being along with his life — and are inseparable from life itself. People cannot be given that which already belongs to them — and only to them.

Here in America, men in public office were to be the recipients, not the donors, of permission. They were to be the servants, not the masters, of the people.

That is what makes the American concept of constitutional government different from that of the British government or that of any other government that had ever gone before. This difference is the essence, the very foundation, of the revolution. Ours is the only basic innovation in political structure since the beginning of recorded history.

That's an important point to remember — especially during these hectic times when the Old World "isms," after a bit of face lifting and relabeling, are being presented in glowing terms as something entirely new and ultramodern. The safety, the freedom, the security, the very life of every American and the future of his children depend upon our understanding the meaning of the *real* revolution.

A Dream Come True

The ten basic amendments were adopted in December, 1791. The dreams of Washington, Franklin, Jefferson, Hamilton, and Madison had become a reality.

From the Old World viewpoint, the Constitution had been too weak before the adoption of the amendments, and now it had been made even weaker. Europeans were aghast. They cried out that this new American government would be short-lived and would come to no good end. The Americans had violated all the experience and wisdom of the ages. Older governments refused to recognize the new federation of states. No government could come nearer to anarchy than this and still be a government.*

*There were dissenters from the European viewpoint, including William Pitt, the English statesman who, after reading the American Constitution, exclaimed that it would be the wonder and

Of course, in the traditional sense of the term, it was not a government. It was a reversal of all the pagan precedents. Instead of following in the footsteps of the Old World dictators by setting up the strongest possible government, the revolutionists had taken exactly the opposite course. Their aim was to make the central government just as weak as possible — throwing the responsibility back on the individual citizens, with the state constitutions serving as buffers.

It must be admitted that the Old World skepticism was not without foundation. Even with the strongest form of government, the prospects would not be bright for the new and sparsely settled states sprinkled along the Atlantic coast, between an inland wilderness and a sea dominated by Great Britain's Navy.

Canada had remained loyal to the King; Spain still held the Floridas, Texas, New Mexico, Arizona, and California; France owned most of the territory between the Mississippi and the Rocky Mountains; Russia was in the extreme Northwest.

admiration of all future generations. And there was Count Aranda who, as Prime Minister of Spain, was trying to bolster its economic affairs and who sounded a note of warning to the Old World monarchies when he said: "This federal republic is born a pygmy. A day will come when it will be a giant, even a colossus."[14]

Chapter 16

UNPLANNED PLANNING

THE states had united in a voluntary federation; but there was no unified control, no over-all plan.

This is just the opposite of the Old World pattern. In other nations, the overlords develop their ambitious plans, enforced by the firing squad and supported by huge predatory armies. These plans look fine on paper, but they are contradictory to the nature of human energy. They are always at the expense of individual initiative; they always result in oppression, leading to human degradation and war.

In America, the planning was to be done on a decentralized, or grassroots, basis. It was a new experiment. Free men were to have an opportunity to live their lives, plan their own affairs, and work with one another — not under the lash of coercive authority, but under the discipline of enlightened self-interest and moral responsibility.

Thus it is that Americans were assured the flexibilities necessary to progress. Thus it is that always in these United States the unintended, the unpredictable, the apparently irrational has seemed to carry us forward. Here are a few examples:

Consider the settlement of Kentucky, for which Richard Henderson and his land company were responsible. Any intelligent man in power would have stopped them in the interest of the general welfare. Kentucky was a wild and lawless country. Already growing too fast, it threatened rebellion against the United States and trouble with Spain.

But Judge Henderson went ahead, and with the aid of Daniel Boone, he organized his company and sold Kentucky land to settlers. He sold it on credit and would have made a tremendous fortune if the settlers had ever repaid him. The rambunctious Kentuckians drove off the installment collectors with guns. The Henderson Land Company went broke. But Kentucky was settled — a full hundred years ahead of schedule!

Consider the Louisiana Purchase, which extended the United States from the Mississippi to the Rocky Mountains. No one in authority had any intention of buying that land. The general feeling was that it was no good, and anyway, there was too much of it. Even the most forward-looking people saw the Mississippi as our permanent western frontier. The great river was a natural geographical boundary. Jefferson himself expressed the view that it would be another 200 years (about 2000 A.D.) before there would be any cities in the Mississippi Valley.

Without Authority

But Kentucky, as predicted, began to make trouble. The isolated western settlers threatened to join Spain, so that they could have a seaport on the Spanish-held Gulf of Mexico. Jefferson saw that the whole West — that is to say, the eastern half of the Mississippi Valley — would be lost unless the United States could get access to the Gulf. All that he wanted was a port, just one little bay.

But in Paris, two American commissioners — on the spur of the moment and without authority from Washington — bought the entire Louisiana territory for $15,000,000.

This wide expanse of territory really belonged to Spain, but Napoleon sold it and took a chance on his armies settling the matter with Spain.

Jefferson was aghast when he heard the news and came within an inch of repudiating the purchase. But the Louisiana Purchase became a part of the United States, and the expansion continued westward.

California was torn from Mexico in a surreptitious personal adventure of General Fremont — connived in by Senator Benton of Missouri, who sent him word to move quickly before he was stopped. At that time, no one dreamed there was gold in those foothills. Thoughtful men pointed out that California's soil was worthless because the United States already had more land than its citizens could use; that for centuries to come, the population on the Pacific coast would not be sufficient to provide a market for its farm products.

No Plan

Everywhere you look in American history, you find examples of things seeming to happen by accident — without intention. Americans had no over-all plan. They had something more important. They had personal freedom to plan their own affairs; and the avalanche of human energy resulting from that freedom swept from the Atlantic to the Pacific, from the Great Lakes to the Rio Grande.

In 75 years, within a man's lifetime, France and Russia

had vanished from the continent. England had been pushed back on the north; Spain had yielded the Floridas, New Mexico, Arizona, California, and Texas.* The whole vast extent of this country had been covered by one nation, a tumultuous multitude of free men — men of heterogeneous races and creeds — living under the weakest government in all the world. The people who had been left to shift for themselves — who had learned the lessons of realism and learned them the hard way — were creating a new world and carrying forward the revolution which was beginning to shake the foundations of the Old World.

---

* I realize that the "Lone-Star" state doesn't belong in this general grouping. With its own revolutionary leaders — its Austins, its Houstons, and its Ebenezer Foxes who died to the last man in the Battle of the Alamo — the story of Texas parallels that of the United States. But since there isn't room in this book to do full justice to the Texans, we'll leave them to work out their own affairs — which, in common with the Cavaliers, they've always managed to do "with engaging gallantry and charm." Ditto California and at least two other states.

Chapter 17

THE REVOLUTION SPREADS

"An army of principles," declared Thomas Paine, "will penetrate where an army of soldiers cannot; it will succeed where diplomatic management would fail: it is neither the Rhine, the Channel, nor the ocean that can arrest its progress: it will march on the horizon of the world, and it will conquer."[13-b]

Many Europeans had joined the Americans during the war, and they carried home the sentiments of Paine — as well as the sentiments of Lafayette, who said: "For a nation to love liberty, it is sufficient that she knows it."[13-c]

And there were converts among the mercenary soldiers who had been brought over from Europe to fight for Britain. Many of them were coming to the same conclusion as the captured Hessian who confided to Paine: "America is a fine, free country . . . I know the difference by knowing my own: in my country, if the Prince says, Eat straw, we eat straw."[13-d] The sentiment for freedom was spreading.

Thirteen years after the Declaration of Independence, the oxcarts and roving hogs were cleared from New York's main street to make way for the inauguration procession of General George Washington, as the first president of the United States of America. Just two months later, a group of freedom-loving Frenchmen declared themselves to be a national assembly and set about to develop a French constitution, patterned after the American model.

Lafayette, with the aid of Jefferson, had carried the revolution to Europe. The people of France adopted the American colors: red, white, and blue. They called their leaders "the Americans" and named General George Washington as an honorary citizen of the new French Republic.

They sent for Thomas Paine and gave him French citizenship. When the news got out, Paine was elected by three different French provinces to serve as their representative at the National Convention. So the author of *Common Sense* sat in the inner councils with Lafayette and the French revolutionists, as they debated their plans and policies — under the American flag and the French tricolor, with portraits of George Washington and Benjamin Franklin gazing down upon them.

Freedom on the March

The initial effort met with reverses, but the new revolution — the *real* revolution — was on the march. During the period 1810-1812, it spread southward in the Western world. There were revolts in Mexico, Venezuela, Argentina, Chile, Paraguay, and Uruguay.

In 1813, Mexico declared its independence from Spain; and in 1819, the people of Colombia took the same action.

Late in 1814, the Treaty of Ghent brought an end to the War of 1812. It was more or less of a draw; but the new American nation had held its own against the might of Britain's Navy, and Americans were no longer molested on the high seas.

In 1822, Brazil proclaimed its independence from Portugal; and in 1890, it was set up as a republic, with its former provinces united under a constitution patterned after ours.

In 1823, the President of the United States announced, through the Monroe Doctrine, that Americans would resist any attempt on the part of the Old World to interfere with revolutionary progress in the Western Hemisphere.

Back in Europe, the struggle for freedom continued with mixed results; and in the 1840's, thousands of defeated revolutionists fled to America. They came especially from Germany, where the fight for freedom seemed hopeless.

In 1848, the Swiss, whose struggle against authority dated back to the legendary period of William Tell, revised their confederation and set up a constitutional republic patterned after the American model, with two legislative bodies — one to represent the different cantons (states), the other to represent the Swiss nation as a whole. Switzerland is really deserving of a special chapter in this book. In common with the Saracens, the Swiss have been neglected by the historical analysts. It is highly significant that their little republic, embedded in the center of Old World conflict, has kept out of the big wars — and the protection afforded by the Alps is only part of the reason.

In the 1850's, Garibaldi, who had been fighting for freedom in South America, carried the revolution to his native land, Italy.

In the 1860's, Americans fought to abolish slavery once and for all. At least, that's usually thought of as the cause of the War Between the States; and it was a just cause, except that the problem of freeing the slaves was already well on the way toward a peaceful solution. But the real issue was the matter of states' rights versus federal domination. Among other things, this involved the tariff question, which had long been a bone of contention between the industrial states and the agricultural states. The latter had for many years been fighting against high tariffs because they violated the principle of no special privileges for any one.

The southern states wanted free ports; the federal government insisted on uniform tariffs at all ports — and the election of 1860 meant *higher* tariffs.

Northerners fought to preserve the American revolution by preserving the Union. Southerners fought to preserve the revolution by defending the rights of the states.

During the War Between the States, European troops moved into Mexico — thus proving that the Northerners were right. But the drifting away from the constitutional balance of power which has been going on ever since may yet prove that the Southerners were right. At any rate, the slaves were freed, and the Declaration of Independence was applied to all.

Lapses

In 1898, Americans went out of these United States to fight for the revolution in behalf of Cuba — against Spanish tyranny. Cuba was freed from Old World oppression, but our federal government took it over.

In that same year, the Filipinos proclaimed their independence from Spain; but instead of supporting their efforts, the United States moved in, fought them for four bloody years, and bought the Philippine Islands from Spain.

While our record is not spotless, these actions were later repudiated. Cuba and the Philippines were released. Since that time, America's attempts to support the cause of freedom in other lands have partially atoned for our earlier lapses into Old World tyranny; but our support would be far more productive if we would do a better job of sowing the seed, instead of merely donating the fruit.

So much for a rapid glance at the first century of the third revolutionary movement.

PART IV

FRUITS OF FREEDOM

Chapter 18

INVENTIVE PROGRESS*

WHEN the American revolution had its beginning, living conditions had scarcely changed since the reign of Nebuchadnezzar. The colonial woman gathered her own firewood and cooked over an open fire, just as women had cooked since the dawn of history, and just as more than two-thirds of the women on earth are cooking today. She spun thread and wove coarse cloth, with a spindle and loom handed down from the early Egyptians. Every housewife made her own soap and candles and carried water from a spring or well. A crude millstone, dating back to ancient Babylon, ground the grain that the American farmer cut and threshed with knives and flails that were older than history.

These were the conditions existing when our forefathers threw off the shackles of Old World tyranny in order that human beings might be in control of their own lives and make full use of their individual initiative.

The outburst of human energy was terrific, and in no way is it better illustrated than by the inventive progress that immediately took place.

In 1793, Eli Whitney invented the cotton gin, which

This chapter is based on material gathered over many years from a wide variety of sources, some of which are listed on page 267. But I especially want to express appreciation to my friend, the late Carl Crow, and to his book *The Great American Customer* (New York: Harper & Brothers, 1943).

[211]

could do the work of four dozen men. But that's only part of the story. Whitney's invention made it commercially profitable to cultivate the short-fiber "green-seed" cotton that grew wild in the foothills of Virginia and the southeastern states. In contrast to the long-staple or sea-island variety, the lint stuck so tenaciously to the short-fiber seed that only a few ounces a day could be separated by hand.

The lower processing costs increased the market for all varieties of cotton. Acreage was greatly expanded, and the southern states entered an era of high prosperity. In less than ten years, the annual production of cotton in America had increased from less than 5,000,000 pounds to over 50,000,000 pounds.

New England shared in this prosperity; the availability of cotton in such large quantities and at such low prices stimulated the development of carding and weaving machinery. A few years later in Waltham, Massachusetts, for the first time in history, raw cotton was turned into finished cloth under the roof of one factory.

Clothing could now be obtained at prices within the reach of all. It was no longer necessary for the housewife to work overtime at her spinning wheel and hand loom. Thanks to Eli Whitney, she could have an occasional evening for rest and recreation.*

*By way of anticlimax, it's disappointing to note that Whitney himself made not one red cent out of the cotton gin. Section VII of the Constitution provided that inventors should, for a period of time, be granted the exclusive right to their original ideas — not so much to protect the inventor, but to make sure that new ideas were made public. As Whitney found, to his sorrow, property rights as applied to inventions were not generally understood. Patents didn't afford much protection on a thing like a cotton gin which could be made in any blacksmith shop.

Mass Production

In 1799, the same Eli Whitney, through the influence of Thomas Jefferson, was given a contract to build muskets for the War Department. His work on that project was one of the most important milestones in the development of modern mass-production technique.

Whitney is frequently spoken of as the inventor of mass production, but that is hardly accurate. In England in the early 1680's, a man named Sir Dudley North had outlined a program of mass production, with particular reference to the building of ships. Sir Dudley's analysis and proposal were presented in a paper entitled *Considerations Upon the East-India Trade*, which stands today as a remarkable document on the fundamentals of mass production.

Sir Dudley was much concerned about the confusion and perplexity to which the workingman was being subjected as a result of his having to switch back and forth from one type of job to another. He wanted to "abate" such unnecessary confusion by advance planning and by assigning jobs of different variety to different artisans of different skills and talents.

No Decrease in Wages

Sir Dudley also foresaw the possibilities of reducing costs "tho' Wages shou'd not be abated."[15] But he was ahead of his time. The idea of increasing production through systematic planning was too revolutionary to be given serious consideration. And the idea of making things easier for the workers was downright anti-social.

Little Progress

A hundred years later, Adam Smith, in *The Wealth of Nations*, expanded on the principles laid down by Sir Dudley North. But mass production had made little headway. Ships were still being built in the old way — with no abatement in the confusion. Production-minded Americans, who probably had never heard of Sir Dudley, were the first to produce ships on a mass-production basis — and they didn't get around to it until World War I.

About all that Adam Smith could find to report along lines of practical progress was that the principle of specialized operation was being applied to the manufacture of dressmakers' pins. That was in the year 1776.

On this side of the Atlantic, in that same historic year, a rumor came out of Rhode Island that a tack maker named Jeremiah Wilkinson had perfected a new invention which would boost his production to several thousand tacks a day per man. Jeremiah's "new invention" turned out to be nothing more than a scheme for fastening a dozen bits of metal in a vise, so that, with a broad-faced hammer, the heads could all be pounded at the same time.

Today such a procedure seems perfectly obvious, but in those days, it was startling news and represented an important step toward modern manufacturing efficiency.

Interchangeability

But mass production, if applied to anything beyond the simplest kind of article, depends not only on division of labor and multiple operations, but also on uniformly accurate, interchangeable parts. Whitney pioneered the idea of interchangeability as a fundamental principle of production, and he successfully applied the principle to a product that must be made with the greatest precision.

Guns had always been built by hand. Each part had to be laboriously filed, lapped, and fitted together by highly skilled gunsmiths. There was no division of labor. No one had ever worried about "abating the confusion." Each worker made everything from the stock to the trigger spring. Each gun was slightly different from every other gun, and each part in each gun was different from the corresponding part in any other gun.

Whitney proposed to substitute highly specialized machine operations for the less uniform hand operations. Thus, each piece would be made exactly as it ought to be in its final form.

Simplified Repairs

This would not only reduce the assembly operation to a routine procedure, but would greatly simplify the problem of repairs. It would no longer be necessary to do a lot of expert filing and fitting to replace a worn or broken part. The principle of interchangeability would make it possible to repair a gun right on the battlefield, without the aid of a professional gunsmith.

Whitney's contract called for the manufacture of 10,-000 muskets over a two-year period; and government officials, thinking in terms of piecemeal or handicraft production, naturally assumed that deliveries would be made at an even rate of about 100 per week. But it is a characteristic of mass production that, while it's a quicker way and a better way to build things once you get started, it takes a long time to get started.*

Around a hundred different machines are required to produce uniform guns on a mass-production basis — not to mention the special tools, jigs, fixtures, etc., that have to be made to order. Even with the highly perfected techniques, facilities, and know-how of today, it would take about six months to buy and install the machinery and equipment needed to produce quality guns on a quantity basis.

But back in 1799, it was not just a matter of going out and buying the machinery. That was before the age of the specialized tool industry. Most of the equipment that Whitney had to have just didn't exist. It had to be designed and built from scratch.

The brilliant, ambitious, and audacious Whitney, unwittingly perhaps, had taken on the job of laying the groundwork for the modern machine-tool industry, without which few, if any, of our manufactured products of today would be available at prices within the reach of the average person.

It would have been much easier to go ahead and make the guns by hand, and presumably the first of them

*As Charles F. Kettering has aptly observed, this is analogous to the publishing business. It takes considerable time to set the type, make the engravings, correct the proofs, take care of make-ready, etc.; but once the presses get going, it's just about as easy to run off a million copies as it is to run off a few thousand. In the printing business, the necessity for all this preliminary work is rather generally recognized, but it is not generally understood that all mass manufacturing involves the same problems — only more so. The story of Whitney has its parallel in the early days of World War II, when industry was being heckled by people who were ignorant of this principle — who thought it was just a matter of turning on the spigot.

were made partly by hand; but at the end of a year, only 500 muskets had been delivered. The War Department was getting impatient and demanded a showdown.

Whitney was summoned to Washington to appear before a committee of experts. He knew he was in for trouble unless he could get them interested in his broad undertaking. He appeared before the committee with a box containing the loose parts for ten guns. Without ceremony, he dumped them on the conference table and, like a jubilant child with a new toy, put on a demonstration of what could be accomplished through the use of special machinery, tools, jigs, and fixtures. With parts chosen at random, and without any filing or fitting, he assembled two guns before their very eyes and passed them around for inspection.

Impressive Demonstration

It was an impressive demonstration, but the committee had to consider the practical aspects. The government had ordered, not ten guns nor 510, but 10,000 guns. The time was half up, and Whitney himself had to admit that he wouldn't be able to meet the schedule. But he fared better than did Sir Dudley North; and with the support of his friend, President Jefferson, the contract was extended.

As time went on, Whitney had to get additional extensions; but the order was finally filled, and the United States entered the War of 1812 with 10,000 of the most perfect muskets that had ever been made. For the first time in history, precision firearms could be produced in almost unlimited quantities.

The War of 1812 was won; and in the years that followed, the conquest and settlement of the West were greatly expedited by Samuel Colt's application of Whitney's techniques.

But of far greater importance, Whitney had laid the foundation for quantity production of complex civilian products — bicycles, typewriters, linotypes, motion picture machines, electric refrigerators, motor cars.

It has been estimated that even the simplest, cheapest, skimpiest kind of automobile could not be built for less than $20,000 without machine tools and the interchangeability of parts which they make possible — and the cost of keeping it in repair would be even further out of line.

Luxurious Gadget

Inspired by what he had learned of Whitney's undertaking, Eli Terry, a clocksmith of Plymouth, Connecticut, announced that he was building 500 clocks — all of the same, identical design — which he would sell for around $10.00 each, as against the customary price of $25.00.

This was even more startling than Wilkinson's new method of making tacks. A tack was a very simple thing; but a clock was a mysterious, delicate, and highly complicated mechanism. Clocks had been built back in the days of the pharaohs, but up to the time of Eli Terry they had always been the ornamental luxuries of kings and princes. The common man had depended on the sun and the stars.

From the Old World viewpoint, time was unimportant, and the conservation of human energy also seemed unimportant. It is only when men are free that they begin to place a value on their time; and when men begin to place a value on human time, they begin to realize the importance of preserving human life.

Down through the ages, the principal business had always been war. When a people won a war, they made slaves of the defeated people; if they lost, they became slaves of their conquerors. In either case, there was always a surplus of burden-bearers. Long hours of drudgery helped to keep the slaves submissive, so there was no incentive to develop labor-saving techniques — no point in worrying about time.

Under such conditions, there was no place for the Eli Whitneys or the Eli Terrys. If any had cropped up, they would have been frowned upon as "enemies of the social order." That is why Sir Dudley's forward-looking ideas were thrown into the discard. Certain of his more daring writings were suppressed until years after his death, when they were published anonymously by a group of cautious admirers.

Terry was no newcomer to the clock business. For some years past, he'd been canvassing the New England countryside, selling high-priced clocks on the installment plan. But the idea of producing clocks of uniform quality at prices low enough to make them available to every family was something new and radical.

Eli Terry, as far as I can find out, was the first to put into practice the American idea of low cost and big volume through mass production and wide distribution. By the end of three years, he and his partner, Seth Thomas, had built and sold over 5,000 clocks.

Others were attracted to the field. Competition increased. Quality improved. Wages went up. Prices went

[219]

down. The unique American formula was in the making!

One manufacturer, a man named Peck, saw possibilities in the export trade. His first shipment of low-priced clocks to England was held up at the Liverpool Customs House on grounds of suspicion. The Customs officials knew the value of clocks, and they knew that clocks just couldn't be produced at the low prices shown on the Peck invoice — fraudulent payments must have been made on the side in order to avoid the full effect of the tariff.

British law provided that under such conditions the goods in question would be confiscated by paying the amount of the invoice plus 10 per cent. The clocks never reached the consignee. They were taken over by the government. What the government did with them, I don't know.

But Peck, being a practical man, didn't put up any argument. He was a hardheaded manufacturer, not a salesman. The 10 per cent extra profit was "pure velvet," and he rather relished the idea of disposing of his output without any sales expense or credit risk. He added more workers and continued shipping his clocks to Britain and collecting from the Customs Office until they finally got wise to him.

Although the records are incomplete, I like to think that the British, at about that time, began to think that perhaps Sir Dudley had something. However, it took another hundred years to develop and extend mass-production techniques to a point where the worker could switch from one job to another without confusion and perplexity.

Sir Dudley's dream was fulfilled — not in England, but here in the United States. It was brought to its fruition through the ingenuity of American production engineers. But scarcely had it reached full perfection when other forms of confusion were injected into the situation. Although of an artificial, man-made nature, they are so befuddling that even a Sir Dudley North might have difficulty in pointing a way to the solution.

6000 versus 160

For thousands of years under the Old World concept of a static economy, operating under bureaucratic control, human beings lived in hunger, filth, and disease. They worked ceaselessly at back-breaking drudgery to keep life in wretched bodies. They died young. For thousands of years, when not fighting wars, they managed to build pigsty shelters, to sow grain, cook meat, yoke oxen, and chain slaves to mills and oars.

Then in this New World, in a brief period of 160 years, Americans created an entirely different mode of life, with improvements and advances in the scale of living beyond the utmost imaginings of all preceding ages. Americans have disproved the pagan superstition of a static universe and have given a new meaning to the word *progress*.

If our progress is to continue, it is important that we do not forget the things which have brought us thus far.

Economists and statisticians are inclined to take the end of the Civil War as the milepost marking the beginning of America's first great era of accelerated progress. In terms of the increased output and higher standard of living, that is true; but the seeds of that progress had been sown by the preceding generations.

Most of the things we have today are traceable, directly or indirectly, to what was going on in the minds of those who were blazing trails 100 and 150 years ago. That's when the basic foundations were being laid, and it is doubtful that there has ever been a time when human energy and original, independent, creative thinking were so intense and so well-directed as in the years immediately following the Revolutionary War.

Elusive Lag

In the progress of a nation, just as in the decline of a nation, there is always a lag between cause and effect. This is an extremely important point, and failure to recognize it seems to account for most of the mistakes and misery of mankind down through the ages. Progress, or lack of progress, at any given time depends on what was happening in the minds of men and women at some previous time. The histories of Greece, Rome, and Spain afford abundant evidence.

Looking to the future instead of to the past, America's progress in the years ahead depends on the American thinking of today. The long range prospects depend, not on us older folks, but on the thinking of the younger people who will be at the helm 10 years, 20 years, 30, 40, 50 years hence.

As individuals, what is their outlook on life? Are they fatalistic or self-reliant? What is the influence of the home, and how does it compare with that of 50 and 100 years ago? What's going on in the schoolroom? What is the philosophy of our educators and of men in public office?

One of the best ways to insure future progress is to keep clearly in mind the things which have been responsible for our past progress, as well as the things which may have kept America from being as great as it might have been.

This chapter is supposed to deal with inventive progress as affecting our economic growth and our high scale of living. And yet I'm not sure that I should apologize for this digression because it all comes back to the effective use of human energy, and the effective use of human energy depends on the mental and moral outlook of the individual persons who make up a society.

Parallel Efforts

As already indicated, it is difficult to trace the "genealogy" of any invention or discovery, and any attempt to do so is accompanied by the danger of omissions and inaccuracies.

Economic needs have a way of permeating society. It is a commonplace in the history of invention to find minds far distant from one another in time and space wrestling with the same problems — working independently but producing results that are roughly identical.

Rarely does anything spring full-blown. Progress advances by degrees, each improvement paving the way for the next; and since the advent of the printing press and the growth of scientific societies, the benefits of the independent efforts have pyramided on one another to an increasing degree and at an accelerated rate.

The more complicated the product, the harder it is to trace the genesis of its development. To tell the story of the steam engine, for example, would take a sizeable volume, with a "begat" chapter as long as the Book of Chronicles.

James Watt is usually thought of as its inventor, and it is true that Watt, more than any other individual, was responsible for the type of engine which ushered in the modern age of power. He introduced the condenser principle and translated reciprocating motion into rotary motion. But steam engines of a crude variety had been used to pump water out of English coal mines before James Watt was born.

As a matter of fact, the principle of the steam engine had been understood back in the days of ancient Greece; and we know that in Alexandria, Egypt, a man named Hero built a steam turbine in the year 130 B.C. But an invention, like a natural resource, doesn't amount to much unless and until something is done about it.

It always takes time to bring an embryonic idea to its full fruition — and the unavoidable lag is often prolonged by well-meaning people who still cling to the pagan concept of a static universe.

The Steamboat

A boat propelled by steam was launched on European waters in the year 1707. It was built by the French scientist, Denis Papin, who was living in Germany at the time. He made a successful voyage down the Fulda River. But at the town of Munden, he was attacked by an organized gang of boatmen. His new contraption was destroyed, and Papin barely escaped with his life. Thus, the pressure groups, through the use of violence, retarded the development of steam propulsion for almost a century. It was in 1807, just an even 100 years after Denis Papin had run afoul of the river gangsters, that Fulton's *Clermont* made its maiden trip from New York to Albany.

Robert Fulton is usually thought of as the inventor of the first American steamboat, but he was more of a promoter than an inventor. No less than 16 steamboats had been built and operated in this country before the launching of the *Clermont*.

Before Fulton

The half-forgotten genius, John Fitch of Bucks County, Pennsylvania, built a steamboat in 1786; and during the following ten years, with the aid of Harry Voight and others, he built five additional steamboats — all of them successful, and each one better than its predecessor.

Fifteen years ahead of Fulton's *Clermont*, Fitch's fourth boat, the *Perseverance*, was operating on a daily schedule up and down the Delaware, carrying passengers between Philadelphia and Trenton, New Jersey. But unlike Fulton, John Fitch was a poor promoter, and he was too engrossed in his work to bother about the political angles.

Then there was the able engineer, Col. John Stevens, who launched his first boat in 1802. His third boat, the *Phoenix* — completed simultaneously with the *Clermont* — was equipped with an improved engine, designed and built by Colonel Stevens himself, whereas the *Clermont's* engine was imported from England.

But Stevens was at a disadvantage because Fulton's backer, Chancellor Livingston, through political pull, had obtained a 20-year monopoly on the operations of steam-boats in and around New York State. Also, it seems that Nicholas Roosevelt, a former associate of Stevens, had thrown his support to Fulton's group.

At any rate, the monopolistic setup was too much for Stevens to buck. So while the *Clermont* was chugging its way up the peaceful Hudson, the Colonel braved the waters of the Atlantic and took his new boat from Hoboken to Philadelphia — the first ocean voyage ever made under steam power.

Livingston and Roosevelt tried to extend their monopoly over the entire United States; but the newly-freed Americans didn't like the idea of governmental restraint — in less than a generation, independent operators had covered the western waters with steamboats of their own contrivance. In the meantime, the dynamic New World had challenged the static Old World by making the first ocean crossing in a boat powered by steam. It was the good ship *Savannah*, which crossed to Cork, Ireland in the year 1818.

Little Things

The demand for houses following the Revolutionary War was as great or greater than it was following World War II.

Lumber was plentiful; the bottleneck was nails. Iron nails had been in use in the Roman Empire at the time of Christ, but they had always been laboriously made by hand; the forging of nails for the building of a house took about as much time as the construction of the house itself. Legend has it that in colonial days old houses were deliberately burned to the ground and the ashes sifted in order to salvage the hand-wrought nails.

Nails sold by the dozen, at prices not much lower than they now bring in antique shops. Thomas Jefferson kept a dozen slaves busy forging nails just to keep up with the building activities on his Monticello estate. But this was all changed when, in 1795, Jacob Perkins of Newburyport, Massachusetts developed a machine that would turn out 60,000 nails a week.

The history of nails is paralleled by that of many other ordinary household items which today are bought at the nearest dime store without a second thought.

The thrifty colonial housewife could have told you without a moment's hesitation just how many pins, needles, and buttons she had in her sewing basket; the head of the house carried a mental inventory covering his meager stock of nails, tacks, screws, and scraps of metal.

Brass buttons sold for ten cents each until Paul Revere, in 1801, worked out a machine that would roll brass of uniform thickness. Then the button manufacturers of Waterbury, Connecticut began stamping out buttons on presses operated by a water wheel.

Pins and needles were especially treasured. They were larger than those in common use today and far more expensive — especially pins, as the heads were made separately and welded or brazed in place. Selling pins "by the paper" didn't come into practice until 1844, when a small manufacturer in Derby, Connecticut worked out a way to produce them entirely by machine at the rate of 2,000,000 a week. Up to that time, ordinary pins sold for as much as 20 cents each and were looked upon as appropriate gifts for weddings and at Christmas time. They also took the place of small change to supplement barter between neighboring families — which, incidentally, is the origin of the phrase *pin money*.

Far-reaching Effects

As in the case of the cotton gin, it is almost impossible to measure the value of any useful invention. The dollar volume of the increased industrial production is only a part of the story and may be greatly exceeded by the gains in human efficiency. Consider the effect of steamships, railroads, telephones, automobiles, airplanes, etc., in releasing time and energy for other purposes. Or, to take a less spectacular example, imagine the time wasted by the colonial housewife in searching for one of her 20-cent pins.

Consider the saving in time and human energy and the thousand-and-one improvements in living that we owe to electricity. Its story is so involved and so far-reaching that it would take a whole book to develop it — even if I had the necessary knowledge and talent for calculations of such astronomical proportions.

But here's just one example, a rather simple example — certainly less spectacular than either electricity or steam power. It has to do with plows.

Plows had been in use since the dawn of history, but they had remained practically unchanged down through thousands of years. At the time of the American Revolution, they were still being made from the prongs of trees, sometimes with a bit of metal fastened to the tip.

It was not the type of problem that appealed to the high-brow scientist. Tilling the soil had always been left to peasants and slaves, so why worry? But in the New World where men were free, a vast agricultural empire was opened up as a result of American ingenuity applied to the improvement of this ancient tool.

In colonial days, the vast midwestern prairie lands and a good part of the Mississippi Valley were looked upon as worthless. Early visitors spoke of the sweeping plains as a "land ocean" that would forever remain wild and uncultivated.

Several Reasons

This conclusion was not without a reason. In fact, it was based on several reasons.

The prairie country, in contrast to the eastern area, was not covered with forests; and although cutting down trees and clearing land had been the bane of their existence, the pioneer settlers looked with suspicion on any land that didn't have to be cleared. They reasoned that if it wouldn't grow trees, it just couldn't be of any value for growing crops.

The prairies were covered by a tough, primeval sod. When this sod was dry, the ordinary plow wouldn't cut through; and when it was softened by rain, the rich loam underneath was so sticky that it clung to the plow blade. The fertile soil of the river valleys was described as "too thick to drink and too thin to plow."

Cast-iron plows had been tried, but without much success. They wouldn't "scour." They were too heavy to handle. And there was an age-old superstition that a plow made of metal would poison the crops.

But John Deere, a Yankee blacksmith who migrated

from Vermont to the Mississippi Valley, was not so skeptical. Instead of using iron, he made a plow out of the very finest steel then available. From an old buzz-saw disc, he trimmed out the required parts; and on patterns carved from a log, he carefully pounded the sheets into the proper shapes and bolted them to a well-constructed hardwood frame.

When you come right down to it, John Deere's plow could hardly be called an invention. About all he did was to find a new use for an old material and to carry out his ideas in a thoroughly workmanlike manner.*

But John Deere's plow cut through the sod like a razor, and the sticky loam slid off the plowshare like butter sliding off a hot knife. True, it was heavier than its wooden predecessor; but John Deere was a giant of a man, and he trudged across the prairie lands with his new-fangled plow thrown over his shoulder, just to overcome the weight argument.

And after John Deere had a few seasons of increasingly

*Years ago, someone down on the farm told me that John Deere invented the knife-edge wheel which runs ahead of the plowshare and makes an incision for it to follow. But that's not true. The rolling colter was in use before the time of John Deere, and his plow wasn't even equipped with one. Indeed, it would be difficult to prove that there was anything entirely original in John Deere's plow. The efforts of other Americans, directed along similar lines, paralleled and even preceded those of Deere. When I ran into these disconcerting facts, I started to throw out the story. Then I thought that perhaps they made it an even better story because it illustrates the very important point that human progress doesn't depend so much on flashes of genius as on the person who does a bang-up job of carrying out his own ideas or the ideas of others. While I am using John Deere's name primarily as a symbol, there can be little argument that he, more than anyone else, was the man who got things started in the prairie "wastelands."

good crops, the realistic, free-minded settlers cast aside the superstition that metal would poison the soil, and the prairie country was on the boom.

Just Reward

A big industry grew out of John Deere's simple invention, and a number of other industries followed in its wake because binders, reapers, tractors, and other advanced types of farm machinery were developed as a natural result of his having found a way to plow the prairie sod.

Millions of acres of the most productive soil in the world were brought into use. Prosperous towns and cities sprang up in the vast prairie "wastelands"; and John Deere's plow, along with the more intricate inventions of Cyrus McCormick and others, opened up similar opportunities for increased agricultural production in all parts of the world — including the Russian Ukraine.

It staggers the imagination to think how John Deere's simple contribution increased the wealth of mankind. Perhaps it would have come without freedom to invent and freedom to share in the rewards of inventive efforts; but there's no escaping the fact that plows had remained practically unchanged down through the ages, while the peoples of the world were going hungry.

I don't know how much money John Deere made as a result of finding a way to plow the rich prairie lands; I doubt if he got any more than he deserved — although I wouldn't attempt to say how much he was entitled to get, nor would I know how to go about estimating it.

I guess one way to do it would be on the basis of how

many hours it took him to think up the idea and to develop the experimental model. The trouble is that inventive genius doesn't operate on an hourly basis. More often than not, worthwhile ideas come in leisure moments, as a result of an interest in the job that extends beyond working hours.

From all I can gather, John Deere had been turning the problem over in his mind for about a year before he hit on the solution. But a year's pay would hardly be enough — even if you figure it on a portal-to-portal basis, at maximum ceiling rates, and triple time for overtime.

Then too, it's quite possible that John Deere may have followed some false leads and spent time on other ideas that didn't "pay off." It might be that some of these futile efforts were the steppingstones which led him to a solution of the plowing problem. But no matter how liberally we might deal with him on an hourly basis, there would be the danger of shortchanging John Deere — and I want no part of it!

Ability to Pay

So let's take another approach and go at it from the standpoint of "ability to pay." Since Deere's sodbuster turned worthless land into highly valuable land, one might argue that he was entitled to a rather liberal percentage of the increased wealth. This might be arrived at by calculating the before and after value of the vast Mississippi Valley — including the fertile farmlands of Illinois, Missouri, Kansas, Nebraska, Iowa, Wisconsin, Minnesota, and the Dakotas, to say nothing of the Russian Ukraine.

Roughly speaking, this represents the area that Jefferson bought from Napoleon for $15,000,000; but when this land was brought under cultivation, the value increased to about $20,000,000,000, which would mean an added wealth of $19,885,000,000.

But that doesn't throw any light on what John Deere's share should have been because it took the co-operative efforts of millions of free men during several generations to provide the follow-through and to get the job done.

True, John Deere played an important part in getting things started; but I'm using his name more as a symbol, and much of the credit belongs to Cyrus McCormick, James Oliver, and other inventors — none of whom could have gotten vary far without the help of still others who supported their efforts. These included those who put up the money to build the factories and equip them with tools; those who used the tools; those who helped to develop new and better tools; those who worked out new and better methods for using the new and better tools; those who contributed to management, distribution, and service; and last but not least, the up-and-coming farmers who were willing to take a chance — to leave their comfortable homes in the East and risk their money, and their lives, to open up a vast new country. I don't know of anyone who would be smart enough to figure their various shares of the increased wealth.

A Tough Problem

It's a tough problem any way you look at it. I guess the only way to solve it is the way it actually was done — through a free and unhampered balancing-out of the incentives and the rewards among the various individuals who played a part. Perhaps it's fortunate that in the days of John Deere, the major emphasis was on increasing wealth, rather than on how it should be divided.

Too much stress on how it should be divided might easily have reduced the amount to be divided because it would have taken more people to do the figuring than to do the job. But that's really getting off the subject; I'm merely trying to emphasize the wealth-producing possibilities of new ideas.

No matter how much money John Deere may have made, it would be insignificant in comparison with the tremendous over-all benefits shared by millions of people. And it's just possible that good old John Deere wouldn't have bothered his head about the plowing problem if he hadn't been living in a free country, where an ambitious blacksmith had a chance to become a prosperous manufacturer. Free minds are inventive minds. That is why America has always been a land of inventors.

Other Inventors

Benjamin Franklin invented a new type of stove which pointed the way to our modern base-burner. He invented the rocking chair and the first pair of bifocal spectacles, and his scientific experiments played an important part in laying the foundation for the great electrical development which took place long after his time. And it was the sly, tolerant, and benign Franklin who invented the American sense of humor, based on the idea: *Don't take yourself or anyone else too seriously.*

Thomas Paine also had an inventive mind. Not only

was he highly creative as a writer and welder of words, but with geometry as his hobby, he also drew up the plans and supervised the construction of the first single-span iron bridge with crisscross struts.

Jefferson's home at Monticello demonstrates his ability as a master of structural design, and the fittings and furnishings disclose many evidences of his mechanical ingenuity. It was Jefferson who designed the first scientifically curved moldboard for a plow. Also, he played an important part in laying the foundation for the more effective administration of patent law, which, as Abe Lincoln later observed, added the fuel of interest to the fire of genius. Since the time of Jefferson, the United States has led the world in the number of patents registered — twice as many as in Great Britain or France and four times as many as in Germany.

In addition to the cotton gin, the modern steamboat, the prairie sodbuster, the reaper, and the binder, Americans invented the sewing machine, the typewriter, the linotype, the telegraph, the telephone, the phonograph, the motion picture, the airplane, the washing machine, the electric refrigerator, and dozens of other electrical appliances.

And Americans developed the techniques of quantity production. In a broad, over-all sense, one might argue that mass production, as we know it in this country, is the most important of all inventions because it is only through mass production that the practical benefits of other inventions can be extended to the millions.

But mass production rests on the foundation of another, and an even greater invention. It is our new and original concept of a political structure based on a principle that is just as true, just as real, just as inexorable as any law of physics — the principle of *individual liberty and freedom*, the principle that each person controls his own life-energy and is responsible for his own acts and for his relationships with others.

This, the first and foremost of all our inventive contributions, is not ordinarily thought of as an invention. But the fact remains that it is the greatest of them all because it serves as the foundation for all the others and provides the opportunity for their full fruition.

Chapter 19

HOPE VERSUS FEAR

No one nation or race of people has a monopoly on creative and inventive talent; but new ideas, like natural resources, don't amount to much unless and until something is done about them. Many of the things we have today are based on inventions of Old World origin. America's first century of industrial progress was largely a matter of getting something done with the half-baked ideas that had been around collecting dust for centuries — while the vast majority of people were doing without.

Inventions and discoveries were being made in the Old World long before the White Man came to America. They are still being made, and they will continue to be made by the few unsquelchable geniuses who, in spite of the static surroundings, persist in their independent thinking — without much hope of reward unless the brain child has military possibilities.

But when creative workers find themselves entangled in artificial restrictions and bureaucratic red tape — in addition to the natural, normal, and unavoidable difficulties surrounding their work — much of the potential talent will die on the vine. Even the irrepressible genius can accomplish very little without the help of others.

To extend the benefits of a new invention or discovery requires complex networks of supporting talents, skills, and physical facilities. Thus, progress in the direction of more and better things for more people depends on maintaining conditions that provide opportunities and incentives extending over a wide area. There must be opportunities and incentives to invent and opportunities and incentives to use; and in between, there must be opportunities and incentives to produce and exchange. Here in America, such opportunities and incentives have been more far-reaching and more favorable than anywhere else in the world.

Freedom of Choice

It all comes back to the matter of individual freedom. We've been free to invent, free to try out new ideas and new methods, free to back up the other fellow's business or go in business on our own, free to take a chance on making a profit or going broke. We've been free to trade with each other over wide areas, free to buy what we please from whom we please — from Maine to California, and from Key West to Seattle.

That, incidentally, is one of the outstanding contrasts between the Old World and the New World. Try to imagine the problems we'd be up against if our country had been set up like Europe, with each state a separate nation, isolated by customs barriers, different languages, and different monetary systems. Contrast that with conditions as they actually are, and remember that we barely escaped following the European pattern.

Absence of trade barriers has kept us away from the strained artificiality of each area's trying to be self-sufficient. This has resulted in logical specialization on the basis of natural resources and climate: cotton in the

South, flour in Minneapolis, movies in Hollywood, and copper mining in Montana.

We've been free to choose our own jobs and free to compete with one another for better jobs, without any overriding authority dictating to us as to where we should work, what we should be paid, and how we should spend it. We've been less afflicted by monopolies, cartels, and restrictive labor organizations than any other country.

There may be exceptions, but I'm inclined to the view that objectionable monopolies cannot exist without the acquiescence of the state — either by unwarranted legal protection or by failure to perform its proper police functions in suppressing commercial gangsterism. I am aware that such transgressions usually result from the efforts of private interests or pressure groups to obtain governmental aid to help them "pull their chestnuts out of the fire." But two wrongs don't make a right. Double guilt lies at the door of those who propose all-out governmental monopoly as a remedy for the lesser evils of the infrequent private monopoly.

A private monopoly can usually be broken in one of two ways: People can stop patronizing it and find substitutes or do without, or the state can force it to dissolve. But government monopoly is *total monopoly;* and since there is no higher power to which to appeal, there is no relief short of rebellion and war. The only safeguard against the evils of monopoly lies in maintaining competitive conditions which provide maximum freedom of choice for the consumer.

Please note that I am not using the term *free enterprise.* This was once a sound term, but the propaganda (both for and against) has given it a pressure-group connotation.

The only sound program for free competitive enterprise — the only program that has a chance to succeed — is one which concerns itself, first, last, and always, with maintaining freedom for the individual citizen — let the chips fall where they may. It's a matter of keeping the way open so that any business or trade group, large or small, may be continually challenged, kept on its toes, even put out of business, by any runner-up who can demonstrate an ability to serve the customer better.

It may be argued, and it frequently is, that free competition is a ruthless and cruel process. But it is not nearly so ruthless and cruel as the opposite philosophy, which down through the ages has kept the majority of people ill-fed, ill-housed, ill-clothed, embroiled in wars, and dying of famine and pestilence.

Hope versus Fear

There is no escaping the fact that human effort is motivated by hope of reward on the one hand, and by fear of punishment on the other. The ideal combination is rewards that are great and reasonably attainable and punishments that are not too severe.

America's economic progress is the result of conditions which have provided maximum opportunities for reward, but which have limited the penalties to personal insecurity and business bankruptcy. At the other extreme is the totalitarian state, which promises security at the expense of freedom and which attempts to "encourage" initiative by the threat of the concentration camp or firing squad.

Under free competition based on personal responsibility and voluntary co-operation, our production of useful goods and services has exceeded anything ever before accomplished. True, we are far from perfect, and in some respects we seem to have been drifting backwards.*

The big point is that our progress to date is the result of an entirely new and different form of political structure which made it possible for human energy and individual initiative to work under their own natural control.

But now let's get away from broad generalities and make a little closer analysis of the effect of political structure on creative thinking and of the benefits growing out of such thinking. For illustrative purposes, we will continue to talk in terms of technical inventions. However, it should be borne in mind that conditions affecting inventive progress in the realm of physics or mechanics have an equal bearing on the development of new ideas and new methods in any field — from statistical techniques to diaper service.

Dynamic versus Static

The inventive mind is an inquiring mind, and the inquiring mind is the mind of a doubter and challenger. Creative thinkers are never satisfied to let well enough alone. They are continually straying off the beaten path and getting out of step with the normal routine. Such people

*To tell the complete story, with all the pros and cons, would take another book; and sooner or later I hope to write such a book, unless someone beats me to it. Among other things, it would include some "thought starters" covering three proposals that might help to reduce the fluctuations in the business cycle.

have no place in an authoritarian society. Even though their explorations may be confined to the area of physical things, there's always the danger of their turning up something that might disturb the planned economy and discredit the superior wisdom of the overlords.

But what's wrong with a government setting up its own bureaus of carefully chosen scientists and inventors to explore new frontiers of progress, under the supervision of those responsible for the over-all planning? Why won't that work?

Part of the answer is that nobody is smart enough to select them. What governmental bureau back in the 1890's would have picked Henry Ford, the powerhouse helper, to pioneer the production of low-priced automobiles? Even his friends and neighbors had him labeled as a scatterbrained tinkerer.*

Who among present-day Washington officials would be able to pick the Edisons and the Ketterings of 25 years hence? Who among the most ardent and self-assured advocates of centralized planning would be so bold as to try to define the next great advance in the realms of scientific development, invention, and production techniques?

Certainly, those assuming the responsibility for mapping out the future would have to consider the disrupting effects of changes due to progress. To ignore the

*And assuming that he had been picked, would his contributions have been as great? Bureaucratic red tape always works at cross-purposes to the development of independent thinking. It saps energy that might otherwise be directed into channels of creative usefulness. Read John Randal Baker's highly significant little book, *Science and the Planned State* (New York: The Macmillan Co., 1945).

necessity of looking beyond the horizon of things already known would make them self-confessed advocates of a static society.

Stubborn Facts

The difficulty lies in the fact that human energy doesn't work according to any foreordained plan or pattern. This is especially true in the field of original exploration. In the higher realms of scientific research, you can't even tell the researcher what to find out — the biggest part of his job is to find out what there is to be found out.

You can't order a person to have an inspiration. Creative ideas spring from within; they can't be forced from without. Genius is an unpredictable quality. It doesn't work according to fixed rules or patterns but turns up in the most unexpected quarters.

Inventive and scientific talent of a high degree can't be produced by bureaucratic edict. Nor can it be discovered through any formalized procedure — the only way it can be done is through *natural selection*. In other words, let the creative mind discover itself. That's the only effective process, and it can only be fully effective in an atmosphere which doesn't prevent anyone from using his own initiative.

As a result of personal freedom here in the U.S.A., the process of natural selection sifts the embryonic geniuses from 145,000,000 people. That's how we found Eli Whitney, Charles Goodyear, Thomas Edison, Michael Pupin, Luther Burbank, Ottmar Mergenthaler, Elias Howe, Samuel Morse, and the Wright brothers. Nobody selected them. Given an opportunity in a free land, they selected

[243]

themselves and forged ahead of their rivals. No governmental bureau can ever compete with this natural process of self-selection on a free and highly competitive basis.

Stimulus

The greater the competition, the better the quality of the persons who reach the top. This is due, not only to the greater number of aspirants, but also to the fact that genius thrives on rivalry. It's not much fun to be an expert in a field which is completely and entirely beyond the understanding of everyone else; nor is there much incentive to widen the gap by becoming even more expert — why increase the loneliness? Galileo would doubtlessly have risen to greater heights if there had been other astronomers, even lesser ones, to criticize and challenge his work on the basis of factual merit.

There is also a highly important, practical, down-to-earth by-product of personal freedom which can only come through the process of competition and natural selection. The maintenance of our American way of life depends just as much on the runner-up as it does on the outstanding genius. Thousands of men of varying degrees of talent and skill are needed to work out the less spectacular details — details which must be taken care of before even the simplest invention or discovery has any practical value for improving the conditions of mankind on a wide scale. Thus the man who doesn't quite win the race is a necessary adjunct to the top-flight genius, who has neither the time nor the temperament to handle the follow-through.

Rewards

The progress and contributions of scientists, inventors, and innovators depend on the opportunities for reward for extra effort. The reward may take various forms. It may be the endorsement of others engaged in the same or similar work. It may be the emotional stimulation resulting from intelligent debate, argument, and criticism from rivals. It may be widespread fame and acclaim — this presupposes some degree of intelligent interest on the part of the general public. Underlying all these is the inner satisfaction of doing a good job; but that's not much of a reward unless it is magnified by recognition from others.

And last, but not least, there is the more tangible form of reward — the pay check or its equivalent. But financial gain is not always the most important incentive. Its importance depends on the individual. Among creative workers, there are those who would find more satisfaction in a complimentary letter from a rival than they would in a salary raise. But the number of Galileos is limited, and even a Galileo can do with some extra cash.

The possibility of fortune, along with fame, insures a bigger crop of geniuses — as well as of runners-up. And in the less dramatic, down-to-earth fields of practical invention and technological progress, the opportunity for financial reward becomes increasingly important as an incentive.

In the final analysis, the size, and hence the effectiveness, of the financial reward — whether it comes through a cash settlement, a royalty payment, a promotion, or a business venture of one's own — depends on the size and vitality of the market for the product or service. Here in America, this vitality is greater than anywhere else. We have less than 7 per cent of the world's population — but we also have the dynamic qualities of 145,000,000 free people.

Here in America, the consumers play a role which extends considerably beyond the function of providing a market. As investors, they supply the tools without which large-scale, economical production with high wages would be impossible. In addition, the consumers provide something else which, although less tangible, is of equal or even greater importance. It is the readiness to try new things — a distinctly American trait, which has a deeper significance than appears on the surface.

Just by way of illustration, I'd like to tell the story of an experience which may help to illustrate the point. In fact, it's two stories, based on two experiences, illustrating several points which started me thinking along these lines.

Some years ago, just before World War II, I read an article on inventions and technical progress. In the early part, it summarized various stories of American inventions and experiments — including the one about Ben Franklin flying his kite during the electric storm, with a brass key attached to the kite string. Considerable emphasis was placed on the fact that many great things had sprung from humble or accidental origin.

That was the general tenor of the first part of the article; but along toward the end, the author began to discuss some theories on over-all social planning. He seemed to forget the unpredictable things that had happened in the past; and in theorizing on the future, he tried to draw some hairsplitting distinctions between useful inventions and nonessential gadgets. He was particularly critical of automobile design and made special mention of the trend toward automatic transmissions as an example of "gadgetry gone wild."

To make a long story short, it added up about like this: At a time when the world was tottering on the brink of disaster, when so many *important* things needed to be done, the automobile industry — prostituting its talents and diverting its engineering genius — was devising gadgets to relieve people of the inconsequential task of shifting gears by hand.

It is quite true that the world was tottering on the brink of disaster, and it is also true that some of the automotive engineers had worked out a way to shift gears automatically. I don't quite agree that it was a useless gadget, but perhaps I am just biased.

The Brink of Disaster

Anyway, my thoughts turned back to Ben Franklin's going out in that storm to fly his kite, and it occurred to me in passing that the world was tottering on the brink of disaster even back in those days. If things had been under "proper control," Mr. Franklin might not have been able to get a priority for the brass key used in his experiment.

That was back in the 1750's, and I'm talking now about the year before Pearl Harbor. The scene shifts to the following year — the summer of 1942, when the world really *was* tottering on the brink of disaster. We and our allies were taking quite a licking in the air, and one of the most urgent problems of military aviation was to outdo our enemies in altitude flying.

Some engineers felt that a hydraulic clutch, similar to the one used in the new automatic transmissions, might help solve the problem. But the idea had been considered quite impractical. A little promotion seemed in order, and I was asked to help write a booklet on the general subject of airplane engines and altitude flying, with a special chapter on superchargers and hydraulic clutches.

Before the book could be published, it had to be passed by the censors. They approved it all right — from the standpoint of military censorship — but they rather questioned the advisability of mentioning the hydraulic proposition. Since, from our standpoint, that was one of the main reasons for publishing the book, we balked a little and asked, *why?*

They explained that the Germans had tried to use the hydraulic clutch in their altitude engine but were giving up the idea. In spite of all their technical skill, the Germans had never been able to make them work properly.

A Successful Gadget

I'll skip the next part of the story, except to say that the booklet was published — and without pulling any punches on the hydraulic clutch proposition. I don't know that the booklet had anything to do with it, but the prejudice faded away; and shortly thereafter, the experience gained in building hydraulic clutches for automobile transmissions was diverted to the building of high-altitude super-superchargers.

A little later, tanks were equipped with automatic transmissions not basically different from those used in some of the present-day motor cars. This made driving a tank so simple that the operator could be trained in a matter of hours instead of weeks. The job no longer called for a muscular giant — and in a pinch, the driver could help with the fighting. Of even greater importance was the fact that the gears could be shifted without bringing the tank to a stop, thus reducing the danger of getting hit. So, in spite of the trouble experienced by the Germans, hydraulic clutches made in American automobile factories played an important part in winning the war, on land as well as in the air.

Adding it all up, my thoughts began to turn back to the article which tried to distinguish between "essential inventions" and "unnecessary gadgets."

And then it dawned on me that the responsiveness of 145,000,000 *free people* provides American industry with a better proving ground than could ever be set up as an adjunct to any factory, in either peace or war. Mass production could never have gotten beyond the experimental stage — in fact, it never could have gotten started — without the support of a public which is alert to progress and which refuses to accept any preconceived boundary between the necessities and the luxuries.

A Contrast

That's an outstanding difference between a free people and a people whose needs, tastes, and desires are regimented in line with some arbitrary, over-all plan. True, the Germans had a lot of trouble trying to make hydraulic-drive superchargers; but America is not Germany. In this country, we don't wait for a war to get experience in the quantity production of precision products. Here in America, around a half-million hydraulic clutches for motor cars had been built before we entered the war. And if we could build them for peacetime use, we could — and did — build them for war!

Thus it is that here in this country the experimenters and the innovators are not confined to the research laboratories, the proving grounds, and the factories. Everyone plays a part, and everyone has a chance. It is impossible to draw any hard and fast boundary lines between the top-flight inventors, the runners-up, the amateurs, the everyday users. No such boundary lines have a chance of staying put. They are shifting back and forth even as this is being written.

In America, to a greater degree than in any other country, there has been the opportunity for self-expression, self-development, and advancement on the basis of merit — regardless of race, creed, or class distinction.

The recognition of the fact that the individual is a responsible human being, free and self-controlling and capable of looking after himself, keeps down the overhead of bureaucratic red tape and the cost of policing. This makes low taxes possible, with the result that any enterprising person may reap a good share of the fruits of any extra effort that he is willing to put forth.

Not having to worry about being robbed of his life, his liberty, or his property, the American has been free to concentrate his energies on the production of useful goods and services. Under such conditions, the habit of thrift has been ingrained. Instead of spending all our earnings on goods for personal consumption, there have been strong incentives to save and invest. The capital resulting from such savings made it possible to build up tremendous resources in the form of more efficient tools of production, thus multiplying the effectiveness of human energy to an unbelievable degree.

Through the extra efforts of millions of people who were willing to work a little harder and to spend a little less than they earned, American workers have been provided with more and better tools than have any other workers in the world, with the result that output and wages are higher here than anywhere else. It has been estimated that our superior tools (mechanical power and laborsaving devices) have expanded our natural human energies to the equivalent of a billion extra workers!

The dreams of Sir Dudley North and Eli Whitney could never have become practical realities except under conditions which provided the incentives to save and invest. Not only have superior tools and equipment made possible the production of more things at lower prices, but also many of the more complex products which we have come to take for granted simply couldn't be made at all, were it not for our highly developed manufacturing facilities.

A Natural Outgrowth

In the last analysis, all of these advantages are the natural, normal outgrowth of a political structure which unleashed the creative energies of millions of men and women by leaving them free to work out their own affairs — not under the lash of coercive authority, but through voluntary co-operation based on enlightened self-interest and moral responsibility.

That's why plows are now made of steel. That's why America has led the world in production accomplishments. That's why we've been able to win wars started by nations that make a regular business of fighting. That's why we are able to feed the victims of pagan aggression.

And last but not least, that's why the people of the United States, who occupy only 6 per cent of the world's land area and who represent less than 7 per cent of the world's population, own:

> 85 per cent of the world's automobiles
> 60 per cent of the life insurance policies
> 54 per cent of the telephones
> 48 per cent of the radio sets
> 46 per cent of the electric power capacity
> 35 per cent of the world's railway mileage
> 30 per cent of the improved highways
> 92 per cent of the modern bathtubs

Before the war, Americans consumed:

> 75 per cent of the world's silk
> 60 per cent of the world's rubber
> 50 per cent of the world's coffee
> 40 per cent of the world's salt.

That last item may sound a bit trivial. I was tempted to leave it out, but some of my economist friends tell me that the amount of salt used is one of the best indications of a nation's production and general standard of living. If so, that statement leads to the startling conclusion that the people of the United States are exactly nine times better off than the people in the rest of the world.

Chapter 20

MORAL VERSUS MATERIAL

THE third attempt to set men free has made the great-grandchildren of the revolutionary leaders the best-fed, the best-clothed, the best-housed, and the most prosperous people on the face of the globe. Many of the things that we have come to take for granted as commonplace necessities of life would have been beyond the fondest dreams of luxury-seeking kings and potentates a few years ago.

Perhaps I'm laying too much stress on material accomplishments, as against the cultural and moral aspects, but I can't see that there are any clean-cut dividing lines. It is generally agreed that the necessities of life must be taken care of before there can be any widespread progress in other, more important directions. But I'd like to suggest that the interrelations are far deeper — that neither the chicken nor the egg comes first.

America's outstanding progress in the realm of material things is the result of an approach which was based on sound moral principles; which threw aside the pagan superstition of a static universe; and which admitted no limitations to man's progress so long as he directs his imaginative abilities and creative faculties in harmony with truth and rightness.

Consider the futile efforts of the ancient alchemist who, laboring under the delusion that things are governed by the whims and fancies of the mythical gods, attempted to change the nature of materials in-the-mass by waving his magic wand and uttering his mystical incantations. His intentions were good, but his beliefs were false; and progress was at a standstill until modern research workers reversed the procedure. In contrast to the ancient alchemist, they delve into the secrets of the molecule and the atom — working from the specific back to the general — with the abiding faith that there is no limit to what can be accomplished, so long as man conforms his plans to the "higher plan" which governs all things.

Voluntary Co-operation

The same principle applies in the fields of industry and commerce. America's accomplishments in quantity production and in the widespread distribution of complex products and services would not have been possible except through the voluntary co-operation of free individuals. This voluntary co-operation depends on the observance of ethical standards based on the recognition of human rights, human obligations, and individual responsibility. It is a practical manifestation of the brotherhood of man, and it is good business. To rely on force and coercion — courts of law and police regulation — is too expensive. It slows things down, adds too much to the overhead, and saps energy that might otherwise be directed to the production of greater abundance.

In the static world of the pagans, the only way to gain a benefit was to take something away from someone else. Under that philosophy, human energy which might have been used to increase wealth was always wasted in fighting over existing wealth. This went on for thousands upon thousands of years; in the process, material wealth was destroyed, human energy was dissipated, and desolation prevailed.

Then, here in America, after 160 years of voluntary co-operation between free individuals, we have pointed the way to a world of peace and plenty. Although we've just barely reached the threshold, we've gone far enough to disprove the age-old superstition that for one person to make a profit, the other must suffer a loss. Under the American formula, the soundness of the Golden Rule becomes increasingly apparent; and for the first time in history, we have witnessed the paradox of higher wages, lower prices, more things for more people — and we're only just getting started!

Not Perfect, But . . .

It is true that America is far from perfect; and being a self-critical and progressive people, we find it easy to visualize a much better world. But in admitting our short-comings and laying our plans to overcome them, there are three questions which might well be asked:

1. To what degree are our shortcomings traceable to the form of political structure under which our country was founded?

2. To what degree are they due to our having drifted away from that concept?

3. How does our record compare with the records of countries which have tried to operate under the opposite philosophy?

And in drawing the comparisons, it's important to bear in mind that we've been at it less than 200 years, as against thousands of years of experience with various forms of regimentation.

Counterrevolutionists

Today we hear a lot of talk to the effect that our original form of government has been outmoded; that it's old-fashioned and needs to be brought up to date; that you can't resist the trend of history; and that we are now in the midst of a new world-revolution.

But the truth of the matter is that the American revolution for human freedom is the only thing that's really new, and it did not end with the surrender of Cornwallis nor with the signing of the Constitution. It's still going on, and the counterrevolutionists — the enemies of freedom — are on the march. Their major attack is not on the open battlefield. It is in the fifth-column technique of skillfully boring from within — a program of infiltration and attrition.

The principal secret weapon is traceable to Lenin, who allegedly instructed his followers to first confuse the vocabulary. Lenin was smart. He knew that thinking can be done only in words and that accurate thinking requires words of precise meaning. Confuse the vocabulary, and the unsuspecting majority is at a disadvantage when defending themselves against the small but highly disciplined minority which knows exactly what it wants and which deliberately promotes word-confusion as the first step in its efforts to divide and conquer.

Lenin was an able strategist, and his instructions have

borne fruit. There are evidences of it on every side. The result is that the communication of logical thought has become increasingly difficult, until today we are living in a world of sugar-coated fallacies, clichés, false meanings, and double talk.

Offhand, one would assume that free Americans, with their unprecedented record of progress, would be completely immune to the propaganda of those who advocate a reversion to pagan ideology. But paradoxically, people who have lived their lives in a civilization founded on Christian ethics are at a serious disadvantage when defending themselves against the surreptitious tactics of those who deny all moral values and who are obsessed with the immoral fallacy, *the end justifies the means*. As Henry J. Taylor expressed it, the best prize fighter, accustomed to following the boxing rules, is not invulnerable when an opponent carries lead in his gloves and has no compunction about hitting below the belt.

The Jujitsu Technique

We in America are up against the problem of protecting ourselves against the jujitsu tactics of those who would have us commit suicide by using our own strength to destroy the very things which are responsible for that strength. Without regard for moral principles of decency and fair play, their techniques are skillfully designed to take advantage of our virtues and to turn them into weaknesses.

Our habit of self-criticism, which is so largely responsible for our progress, makes us particularly vulnerable to distorted propaganda which exaggerates our deficiencies and holds out false promises of a short cut to the millennium. Thus it is that some of our most patriotic, high-minded, and well-meaning citizens succumb to the overtures of those who would make them the innocent tools of subversion.

The fact that we are a progressive and open-minded people, always on the alert for new ideas, makes us susceptible to old ideas when they are attractively camouflaged and presented as something new.

Being a hospitable, tolerant, and fair-minded people, we are inclined to consider both sides of every question. That's all right up to a point, *but when it comes to the eternal verities of moral truth, there are no two sides to the question.* Right is right, and wrong is wrong; and any concession to the pagan viewpoint — whether in the name of expediency or open-mindedness — paves the way for the destruction of all moral values.

Look at the Record

I repeat that America is far from perfect. It would be easy to write a whole book on the negative aspects; but in recent years, that side has been so overstressed that I make no apology for concentrating on the doughnut instead of on the hole. On any honest basis of comparison, the record of America speaks for itself.

In this republic, less than 7 per cent of the earth's population has created more new wealth than all the other 2,010,000,000 people in the world; and the benefits of this great wealth have been more widely distributed here than in any other country — at any time. In addition to, or rather as a result of, such accomplishments, we have more churches, more schools, more libraries, more recreational facilities, more hospitals. Americans have gone further than any other people in the elimination of abusive child-labor practices, the reduction of back-breaking drudgery, the spread of literacy, enlightenment, health, longevity, general well-being, and good will toward others.

Ours is the only continent on which there has never been a general famine. Aside from the early settlers, few people in America ever have gone hungry. Even in the depths of our worst depression, Americans who were on relief were living better than most of the fully-employed in other countries.

There is more laughter and more song in these United States than anywhere else on earth. In shops, streets, factories, elevators, on highways and on farms — everywhere — Americans are friendly and kindly people, responsive to every rumor of distress. Someone in America will always divide his food and share his gasoline or his tire tool with a person in need.

It would seem that insecurity, the price of freedom, has bred a degree of human sympathy that is without parallel in the history of mankind. It is only in America that rank-and-file citizens, over and over again, have made millions of small sacrifices in order to pour wealth over the rest of the world, to relieve suffering in such faraway places as Armenia, Russia, China, and Japan.

Opportunities

With the shortest working hours on earth, we have greater opportunities for self-improvement and personal advancement. But please note that the emphasis is on the word *opportunities*. The matter of taking advantage of opportunities is up to the individual. It cannot be otherwise. There are no substitutes for self-faith, self-reliance, self-development, individual effort, and personal responsibility. Life is no bed of roses. The end of man is not self-indulgence, but achievement. There are no short cuts, no substitutes for work.

Human life came into being and aspires to advance in the face of conflict, struggle, pain, and death. In the last analysis, no person's security can exceed his own self-reliance; when anyone denies this self-evident truth, the chances are that he has for too long depended on someone else to do his fighting for him.

If, down through the ages, men and women hadn't stood up to the job of living — if they hadn't taken risks, faced dangers, suffered exhaustion beyond exhaustion, and kept on fighting and working in the faint hope of victory — then there would be no human being left to tell the story.

Living is a tough job. Only good fighters can make a go of it. The tragedy is that we waste our energies in fighting one another, instead of fighting the common enemies of mankind — famine, pestilence, disease, and other destructive forces of the nonhuman world.

Chapter 21

FREEDOM VERSUS WAR

UNDER the pagan fallacy of a static universe in which new wealth cannot be created, the only way to gain an advantage is to take something away from someone else. When men are free, they soon learn that wars of aggression are unprofitable; that human energies are far more productive when applied to the peaceful pursuits of creating and exchanging useful goods and services.

But when war is forced upon them, they always give a good account of themselves. The reasons for this are not far to seek:

1. Military strength rests on a foundation of economic strength.

2. Economic strength depends on the number of people engaged in productive work, as against the number on public payrolls.

3. Free individuals have greater initiative. They are more ingenious and more resourceful in adapting themselves to the emergencies of war and in matching wits with the aggressors — from a military standpoint as well as from a technological standpoint.

4. They have more to fight for and do not need to be egged on by spurious propaganda.

Force and Trickery

From Genghis Khan to Adolf Hitler, the standard practice in the Old World has been to appropriate the goods of others through the use of brute force. To justify their aggression, those in authority have used propaganda designed to frighten their subjects into believing that they are surrounded by enemies about to attack.

Under their gods of superstition – the will-of-the-swarm, the despots, the dictators, and the führers – the peoples of Europe and Asia have carried on an almost uninterrupted war since the beginning of history. During the past 30 centuries, for example, only one year out of every 15 has been free from war; and even in the brief intervals of peace, the preparations for war have sapped energy which might otherwise have been directed toward constructive pursuits. Imagine what kind of world this would be if the energies of its 2,155,000,000 people were removed from war efforts, freed from bureaucratic regimentation, and applied to the invention, production, and exchange of useful goods and services.

The Cause of War

Down through the ages, human beings have always tried to stop war by utterly crushing the enemy. There has been no progress, for the simple reason that the underlying cause of war is *not* the enemy. Combat on the battlefield is merely a symptom. War is caused by a false notion of human energy, based on the ancient superstition that men and women should be reduced to the status of the beehive. When the majority of people on this

[262]

earth come to realize that they are free, self-controlling, responsible for their own acts and for their relationships with others, there will be no war.

Until that time, Americans must continue to lead the struggle against the forces of paganism — in time of peace as well as in time of actual war. We've always given a good account of ourselves on the battlefield, and we've played an important role as the arsenal of democracy — or rather, as the arsenal of freedom. The victims of paganism always look to America for help in fighting off their aggressors. And America always plays the major role in helping its friends, as well as its enemies, to get back on their feet.

But there are definite limits to how far we can go in that direction. Perhaps we would be doing the peoples of the world a greater and more enduring service if, along with each item of food, clothing, money, and equipment, we sent a simple, matter-of-fact statement of the reasons underlying our ability to make contributions which are so far out of proportion to our population and our natural resources.

And I rather like this idea from another standpoint. In the role of salesmen for America, perhaps we might become more appreciative of our own product, more steadfast in holding to the faith of our fathers, more alert in resisting the alluring promises of false Utopias, which for over 6,000 years have kept the vast majority of people underfed, poorly clothed, embroiled in wars, and surrounded by famine, pestilence, and human degradation.

THE END

APPENDIX

REFERENCES

1. Isabel Paterson, *The God of the Machine* (New York: G. P. Putnam's Sons, 1943), chap. xx.
   a. p. 155.
2. *Plutarch's Lives* (Chicago: Henry Regnery Co., 1949), pp. 33-34.
3. Rose Wilder Lane, *The Discovery of Freedom* (New York: The John Day Co., 1943), pp. 7-8.
   a. pp. 20-21.
   b. pp. 110-111.
   c. p. 120.
4. William Cobbett, *Cobbett's Parliamentary History of England from the Norman Conquest in 1066 to the Year 1803.* (London: R. Bagshaw, 1808), Vol. IV, p. 291.
5. Henry Thomas Buckle, *History of Civilization in England,* (2nd London Ed.; New York: D. Appleton & Co., 1874), Vol. I, pp. 201-202.
6. Thomas Carlyle, *Heroes and Hero Worship* (Chicago: A. C. McClurg & Co., 1897), p. 93.
7. Harold Lamb, *The Crusades: Iron Men and Saints* (Garden City, N. Y.: Doubleday, Doran & Co., 1930), p. 214.
8. George Sale (trans.), Mohammed's *The Koran* (Boston: T. O. H. P. Burnham, 1862), pp. 73, 81.
9. Vilhjalmur Stefansson, *Great Adventures and Exploration* (New York: The Dial Press, 1947).
10. Samuel Eliot Morison, *Admiral of the Ocean Sea* (Boston: Little, Brown & Co., 1942), p. 206.
    a. p. 571.
11. David Saville Muzzey, *History of the American People* (Boston: Ginn & Co., 1938), p. 65.
12. Ebenezer Fox, *The Adventures of Ebenezer Fox, in the Revolutionary War* (Boston: Charles Fox, 1838).
13. Philip S. Foner (ed.), *The Complete Writings of Thomas Paine,* 2 vols. (New York: The Citadel Press, 1945), Vol. I, p. 45.
    a. Vol. I, p. 50.
    b. Vol. I, p. 622.
    c. Vol. I, p. 255.
    d. Vol. I, p. 322.
14. John Fiske, *The Critical Period of American History* (Boston and New York: Houghton, Mifflin & Co., 1898), p. 19.
15. Sir Dudley North, *Considerations Upon the East-India Trade* (London: A. & F. Churchill, 1701), p. 68.

BIBLIOGRAPHY

The mere mention of books that have been used for reference purposes and as stimulants to thought, can indicate only a small part of one's obligation to those who have specialized in areas so vast as those touched upon in *Mainspring*.

As will be noted, the list includes some items that are opposed to the philosophy of individual freedom and which are not recommended—*except for antitoxin effects*.

Adams, James Truslow. *The Living Jefferson.* New York: Charles Scribner's Sons, 1936.

Adams, William Henry Davenport. *Warriors of the Crescent.* New York: Appleton-Century-Crofts, Inc., 1892.

Ali, Ameer. *Short History of the Saracens.* New York: The Macmillan Co., 1943.

Andrews, Matthew Page. *Social Planning by Frontier Thinkers.* New York: Richard R. Smith Publisher, 1944.

Ballinger, Willis J. *By Vote of the People.* New York: Charles Scribner's Sons, 1946.

Bancroft, Charles. *Footprints of Time and Analysis of our American Government.* Washington, D. C.: R. T. Root Publishing Co., 1878.

Beard, Charles A. *A Basic History of the U. S.* Garden City, N. Y.: Doubleday and Co., Inc., 1944.

————. (ed.) *Century of Progress.* New York: Harper and Brothers, 1932.

Beard, Charles A. and Mary R. *The Rise of American Civilization.* New York: The Macmillan Co., 1937.

Belloc, Hilaire. *The Crises of Civilization.* New York: Fordham University Press, 1937.

————. *The Crusades.* Milwaukee: Bruce Publishing Co., 1937.

————. *Great Heresies.* New York: Sheed and Ward, 1938.

Borth, Christy. *Masters of Mass Production.* Indianapolis: The Bobbs-Merrill Co., Inc., 1945.

————. *Pioneers of Plenty.* Indianapolis: The Bobbs-Merrill Co., Inc., 1939.

Boyd, Thomas A. *Research, the Pathfinder of Science and Industry.* New York: Appleton-Century-Crofts, Inc., 1935.

Brant, Irving. *James Madison, The Virginia Revolutionist.* Indianapolis: The Bobbs-Merrill Co., Inc., 1941.

Brebner, J. B. *Explorers of North America 1492-1806.* New York: The Macmillan Co., 1933.

Burckhardt, Jacob. *Force and Freedom.* New York: Pantheon Books, Inc., 1943.

Burgess, John W. *Reconciliation of Government with Liberty.* New York: Charles Scribner's Sons, 1915.

Burlingame, Roger. *Engines of Democracy.* New York: Charles Scribner's Sons, 1940.

————. *March of the Iron Men.* New York: Charles Scribner's Sons, 1942.

Burnham, James. *The Managerial Revolution.* New York: The John Day Co., 1941.

————. *Struggle for the World.* New York: The John Day Co., 1947.

Byng, Edward. *World of the Arabs.* Boston: Little, Brown and Co., 1941.

Carroll, Mary T. *The Man Who Dared to Care.* New York: Longmans, Green and Co., Inc., 1942.

Carver, Thomas Nixon. *Essays in Social Justice.* Cambridge: Harvard University Press, 1915.

Chase, Ellen. *The Beginnings of the American Revolution.* New York: Baker and Taylor, 1910.

Clark, Fred G. and Rimanoczy, Richard Stanton. *How We Live.* New York: D. Van Nostrand Co., Inc., 1944.

Clark, Fred G. *Magnificent Delusion.* New York: McGraw-Hill Book Co., 1940.

Clark, Victor S. *History of Manufacture in the U. S.*, Vol. I. New York: McGraw-Hill Book Co., 1929.

Commager, Henry Steele and Morison, Samuel Eliot. *Growth of the American Republic.* 3rd ed. New York: Oxford University Press, 1942.

Cooper, Harriet C. *James Oglethorpe.* New York: Appleton-Century-Crofts, Inc., 1904.

Crevecoeur, H. St. John de. *Letters from an American Farmer Describing Customs of the British Colonies in North America.* London: T. Davies, 1782.

Crowther, Samuel. *Time to Inquire.* New York: The John Day Co., 1942.

Dampier, William. *A History of Science.* New York: The Macmillan Co., 1943.

Drucker, Peter F. *The Future of Industrial Man.* New York: The John Day Co., 1942.

Dunbar, Seymour. *History of Travel in America.* New York: Tudor Publishing Co., 1915.

du Noüy, Lecomte. *Human Destiny.* New York: Longmans, Green and Co., Inc., 1947.

Durant, Will. *The Life of Greece.* New York: Simon and Schuster, Inc., 1939.

Edmunds, Sterling Edwin. *Struggle for Freedom.* Milwaukee: Bruce Publishing Co., 1946.

Elliott, Jonathan. *Debates on the Adoption of the Federal Constitution.* Philadelphia: J. B. Lippincott Co., 1896.

Fischer, Martin. (trans.) *Gracian's Manual on the Art of Worldly Wisdom.* Springfield, Ill.: Charles C. Thomas, Publisher, 1934.

————. *In Praise of Man.* Springfield, Ill.: Charles C. Thomas, Publisher, 1943.

Flynn, John T. *As We Go Marching.* Garden City, N. Y.: Doubleday and Co., Inc., 1944.

Frazer, Sir James. *Golden Bough.* New York: The Macmillan Co., 1930.

Fuller, Claud E. *The Whitney Firearms.* Huntington, W. Va.: Standard Printing and Publishing Co., 1946.

Garrett, Garet. *The Revolution Was.* (pamphlet) Caldwell, Idaho: Caxton Printers, Ltd., 1944.

Gideonse, Harry David. *Organized Society and Public Policy.* (pamphlet) Chicago: University of Chicago Press, 1939.

Gilman, Arthur. *Story of the Saracens.* New York: G. P. Putnam's Sons, 1891.

Hankin, Hanbury. *Common Sense and Its Cultivation.* New York: E. P. Dutton and Co., Inc., 1926.

Hardy, Edward Rochie Jr. *Militant in Earth.* New York: Oxford University Press, 1940.

Harper, Floyd A. *Freedom and Enterprise.* (pamphlet) Irvington-on-Hudson, N. Y.: The Foundation for Economic Education, Inc., 1945.

Harris, Joel Chandler. *Stories of Georgia.* New York: American Book Co., 1896.

Hayek, Friedrich A. *The Road to Serfdom.* Chicago: University of Chicago Press, 1944.

Hazlitt, Henry. *Economics in One Lesson.* New York: Harper and Brothers, 1946.

Hitler, Adolf. *Mein Kampf.* New York: Reynal and Hitchcock, 1940.

Hogben, Lancelot. *Science for the Citizen.* New York: Alfred A. Knopf, Inc., 1938.

Holbrook, Stewart H. *Lost Men of American History.* New York: The Macmillan Co., 1946.

Houghton, Walter. *Kings of Fortune.* Chicago: Loomis National Library Assn., 1888.

Howe, E. W. *Ventures in Common Sense.* New York: Alfred A. Knopf, Inc., 1921.

Hunt, Betty Knowles. *Show Me Any Other Country.* (pamphlet) Irvington-on-Hudson, N. Y.: The Foundation for Economic Education, Inc., 1947.

Jaffe, Bernard. *Men of Science in America*. New York: Simon and Schuster, Inc., 1944.

Japp, Alexander H. *Master Missionaries*. New York: Robert Carter and Brothers, 1881.

Kaempffert, Waldemar. (ed.) *A Popular History of American Inventions*. New York: Charles Scribner's Sons, 1924.

Kay-Scott, C. (Frederick Creighton Wellman). *Life Is too Short*. Philadelphia: J. B. Lippincott Co., 1943.

Keary, C. F. *Vikings in Western Christendom*. New York: G. P. Putnam's Sons, 1891.

Knight, Lucian Lamar. *Georgia's Landmarks, Memorials and Legends*. Atlanta: The Byrd Printing Co., 1913.

Lane, Rose Wilder. *Give Me Liberty*. (pamphlet) New York: Lew Ney, 1945.

Lawrence, T. E. *Seven Pillars of Wisdom*. Garden City, N. Y.: Doubleday and Co., Inc., 1935.

Le Vert, Octavia Walton. *Souvenirs of Travel*. New York: S. H. Goetzel and Co., 1857.

Link, Henry C. *Rediscovery of Man*. New York: The Macmillan Co., 1938.

————. *Rediscovery of Morals*. New York: E. P. Dutton and Co., Inc., 1947.

————. *Return to Religion*. New York: The Macmillan Co., 1936.

Lippmann, Walter. *The Good Society*. Boston: Little, Brown and Co., 1943.

Lodge, Henry Cabot. *The Works of Alexander Hamilton*. New York: G. P. Putnam's Sons, 1904.

Mackay, Charles. *Extraordinary Popular Delusions and the Madness of Crowds*. Boston: L. C. Page and Co., 1932.

Marx, Karl. *Capital*. Chicago: Charles H. Kerr and Co., 1906.

Marx, Karl and Engels, Friedrich. *Communist Manifesto*. Many editions available.

Masse, Henri. *Islam*. Translated from the French by Halide-Edib. New York: G. P. Putnam's Sons, 1938.

McIlwain, Charles Howard. *Constitutionalism, Ancient and Modern*. Ithaca, N. Y.: Cornell University Press, 1940.

McIntire, Carl. *Rise of the Tyrant*. Collingswood, N. J.: Christian Beacon Press, 1945.

Mencken, Henry L. and LeMonte, Robert R. *Men versus the Man*. New York: Henry Holt and Co., 1910.

Mencken, Henry L. *A New Dictionary of Quotations*. New York: Alfred A. Knopf, Inc., 1942.

Miller, John Chester. *Origins of the American Revolution*. Boston: Little, Brown and Co., 1943.

Mises, Ludwig von. *Bureaucracy*. New Haven: Yale University Press, 1944.

————. *Planned Chaos*. Irvington-on-Hudson, N. Y.: The Foundation for Economic Education, Inc., 1947.

Mosca, Gaetano. *The Ruling Class*. New York: McGraw-Hill Book Co., 1939.

Mussolini, Benito. *My Autobiography*. New York: Charles Scribner's Sons, 1928.

Nock, Albert Jay. *Our Enemy the State*. Caldwell, Idaho: Caxton Printers, Ltd., 1946.

Norton, Thomas James. *The Constitution of the United States — its Sources and its Applications*. New York: America's Future, Inc., 1951.

Oliver, Frank J. *The Machine Tool Primer*. Newark, N. J.: The Herbert D. Hall Foundation, 1943.

Oliver, F. S. *The Endless Adventure*. Boston: Houghton Mifflin Co., 1931.

Ortega y Gasset, Jose. *The Revolt of the Masses*. New York: W. W. Norton and Co., Inc., 1932.

Patric, John. *Yankee Hobo in the Orient*. Frying Pan Creek, Oregon: John Patric, 1945.

Pettengill, Samuel. *Jefferson, the Forgotten Man*. New York: America's Future, Inc., 1938.

Pirenne, Henri. *Mohammed and Charlemagne*. New York: W. W. Norton and Co., Inc., 1939.

Pitkin, Walter B. *A Short Introduction to the History of Human Stupidity.* New York: Simon and Schuster, Inc., 1932.

Pool, John J. *Studies in Mohammedanism.* London: Archibald Constable and Co., 1892.

Pound, Arthur. *The Iron Man in Industry.* Boston: Atlantic Monthly Press, 1922.

Prentice, E. P. *Hunger and History.* New York: Harper and Brothers, 1939.

Queeny, Edgar Monsanto. *The Spirit of Enterprise.* New York: Charles Scribner's Sons, 1943.

Read, Leonard E. *Pattern for Revolt.* (pamphlet) New York: Press of Joseph D. McGuire, 1948.

Robnett, George Washington. *Can We Preserve Our American System in the Post-War World?* Chicago: National Laymen's Council.

Roosevelt, Franklin Delano. *Public Papers and Addresses.* New York: Random House, 1938.

Rucker, Allen. *Labor's Road to Plenty.* Boston: L. C. Page and Co., 1937.

Russell, Bertrand. *Mysticism and Logic.* New York: W. W. Norton Co., Inc., 1929.

Ryder, A. W. (trans.) *Bhagavad-Gita.* Chicago: University of Chicago Press, 1929.

Scherman, Harry. *The Promises Men Live By.* New York: Random House, 1938.

Simons, Henry C. *A Positive Program for Laissez Faire.* (Public Policy Pamphlets.) Chicago: University of Chicago Press, 1934.

Smith, Adam. *The Wealth of Nations.* New York: E. P. Dutton and Co., Inc., 1776.

Snyder, Carl. *Capitalism the Creator.* New York: The Macmillan Co., 1940.

Sparks, W. H. *The Memories of Fifty Years.* Philadelphia: Claxon, Remsen and Hoffelfinger, 1870.

Spears, John R. *American Slave-Trade.* New York: Charles Scribner's Sons, 1900.

Spengler, Oswald. *The Decline of the West.* Translated by Atkinson. New York: Alfred A. Knopf, Inc., 1932.

Stamp, Sir Josiah. *Motive and Method in a Christian Order.* New York: Abingdon - Cokesbury Press, 1936.

Stephens, Alexander H. *Constitutional View of the Late War Between the States.* Philadelphia: National Publishing Co., 1868.

Sumner, William Graham. *Folkways.* Boston: Ginn and Co., 1906.

——————. *The Forgotten Man.* (pamphlet) New Haven: Yale University Press, 1918.

Taylor, Frederick Winslow. *The Principles of Scientific Management.* New York: Harper and Brothers, 1916.

Taylor, Henry J. *Men and Power.* New York: Dodd, Mead and Co., 1946.

——————. *Men in Motion.* Garden City, N. Y.: Doubleday and Co., Inc., 1943.

Thorndike, E. L. *Human Nature and the Social Order.* New York: The Macmillan Co., 1940.

Turner, John K. *Challenge to Karl Marx.* New York: Reynal and Hitchcock, 1941.

Usher, Abbott F. *History of Mechanical Inventions.* New York: McGraw-Hill Book Co., 1929.

Van Doren, Carl. *Benjamin Franklin.* New York: The Viking Press, 1938.

Vreeland, Hamilton. *Twilight of Individual Liberty.* New York: Charles Scribner's Sons, 1944.

Wallace, Henry Agard. *The American Choice.* New York: Reynal and Hitchcock, 1940.

Watts, Vervon Orval. *Do We Want Free Enterprise?* Los Angeles: Los Angeles Chamber of Commerce, 1944.

——————. *Why Are We So Prosperous?* Minneapolis: Burgess Publishing Co., 1938.

West, Willis Mason. *Modern World, from Charlemagne to the Present Time.* Boston: Allyn and Bacon, 1915.

Wilder, Laura Ingalls. *The Little House Series.* New York: Harper and Brothers, 1940.

Woodward, W. E. *Tom Paine, America's Godfather.* New York: E. P. Dutton and Co., Inc., 1945.

Woodward, W. H. *Short History of the Expansion of the British Empire.* New York: Cambridge University Press, 1899.

Wright, Robert. *Memoir of General James Oglethorpe.* London: Chapman and Hall, 1867.

Wyer, Samuel S. *America's Opportunity for Greatness* (1946). *Shift of Civilization* (1929). *Struggle for Bill of Rights* (1945). Pamphlets, privately printed: 1325 Cambridge Blvd., Columbus 8, Ohio.

Zinsser, Hans. *Rats, Lice and History.* Boston: Little, Brown and Co., 1935.

Encyclopaedia Britannica. (14th Edition) Chicago: Encyclopaedia Britannica, Inc., 1929.

Great Events by Famous Historians. (United Empire Edition, 20 vols.) London, Eng.: The National Alumni, 1905.

EDITOR'S NOTE

For additional references to libertarian literature, readers may wish to consult the following bibliographies prepared since the first publication of *Mainspring.*

Harper, F. A. *A Bibliography on the Voluntary Society.* Irvington-on-Hudson, N. Y.: Foundation for Economic Education, Inc., 1953.

One hundred selected titles in economics, history and philosophy. (8 pages, multilithed)
Also available are brief reviews of these works with biographical data about the authors, as prepared by Mary Homan Sennholz.

Hazlitt, Henry. *The Free Man's Library.* Princeton, New Jersey: D. Van Nostrand Company, Inc., 1956.

A descriptive listing of more than 550 outstanding books on the philosophy of individualism, free trade, free enterprise, free markets, and individual liberties.

INDEX

* Asterisks refer to footnotes.

40901